Jeff Galloway

Fit Kids – Smarter Kids

Avonli, Anjoli
& Aliyah

Keep exercising!

FIT KIDS
SMARTER KIDS

JEFF GALLOWAY

MEYER
& MEYER
SPORT

British Library Cataloguing in Publication Data
A catalogue record for this book is available from the British Library

Jeff Galloway: Fit Kids – Smarter Kids
Oxford: Meyer & Meyer Sport (UK) Ltd., 2007
ISBN 10: 1-84126-193-9
ISBN 13: 978-1-84126-193-5

© 2007 by Meyer & Meyer Sport (UK) Ltd.
Aachen, Adelaide, Auckland, Budapest, Graz, Johannesburg,
New York, Olten (CH), Oxford, Singapore, Toronto
Member of the World
Sports Publishers' Association (WSPA)
www.w-s-p-a.org
Printed and bound by: B.O.S.S Druck und Medien GmbH, Germany
ISBN 10: 1-84126-193-9
ISBN 13: 978-1-84126-193-5
E-Mail: verlag@m-m-sports.com
www.m-m-sports.com

CONTENTS

- **Section IV: A Guidebook for Parents, Teachers, Youth Leaders**

- **Section V: Nutrition & Fat Burning**

- **Success Stories**

- **Successful Programs**

- **Troubleshooting**

INTRODUCTION

Every Kid Can Be A Fit Kid
...and a More Successful Adult

"When done correctly, exercise produces a joy that enhances quality of life at any age"

Today's kids are under a serious health threat and yet many parents and teachers are letting them slide into ripe conditions for degenerative diseases. If not recognized and addressed, many of the kids in our community will suffer significant health problems as young adults, resulting in reduced opportunities and premature deterioration of life itself. While many children are already on the path to degenerative disease, by taking action now, thousands of kids can turn this situation around.

Due to sedentary lifestyle and poor nutrition, today's children are the least fit and the most fat of any generation on record. Experts who predict longevity, believe that these youngsters could be the first generation that does not live as long as their parents. More troubling is the fact that by letting children become sedentary and fat, we are setting them up for failure. You'll see in the research section of this book that overweight/sedentary kids have a much greater chance of degenerative diseases, much earlier in life. They tend to have less confidence, do more poorly in school and are less successful as adults. Do you want to allow this to happen to the kids in your family, or class?

This book offers a turnaround strategy. I know that it is possible because, at 13, I was a fat, sedentary kid myself. I had tasted exercise in physical education classes, didn't like it, and searched for the lowest level of exertion I could get away with in exercise and academics. Because of a requirement that I enroll in a sports activity after school when I was 13, I chose track conditioning. My lazy friends were surprised but the decision was very logical, based on the options: 1) Being on the swimming team meant driving across town, and getting home very late. 2) I was terrible at basketball and didn't want the other players to make fun of me. 3) The kid grapevine told me that the track coach was the most lenient teacher and coach in the school. According to reports from a lethargic student who had participated in this, you could run from the track to the woods (less than 200 yards), hang out with other lazy kids throwing rocks into the creek, and jog back at the end of the period. At the time, my grades ranked me in the lower half of the class.

As fate would have it, I fell in with several members of the cross country team (the group in school with the highest grade point average) who I liked and who actually enjoyed running. At first I enjoyed the jokes, gossip, and interplay of personalities—even though the running was tough. Week by week I found myself getting better in every way. Most of the runs were non-competitive and fun. As my peer group changed, I expected more out of myself in fitness and in class. A few semesters later, I made the honor roll.

This book is a guide for parents, teachers, youth leaders, and anyone who wants to help kids become more active, and make better food choices. Because much of the learning comes from following an example, I'm asking that each parent or leader make a commitment to regularly exercise. This will not only show the kids you're serious about the benefits. Like the fit kids, you'll improve your attitude and vitality; you'll also relieve stress, while statistically extending your lifespan. Best of all—you'll feel better.

The mission of this book is to give kids and adults the tools to take control over their fitness, their nutrition, their energy level and their attitude. The result is better control over your life. You'll find inside an explanation of the processes that produce health and good nutrition, and the endless stream of benefits that come to those who regularly exercise and eat correctly.

Most kids want to be fit kids

Almost every child wants to move around, run, jump, exert him or herself, and glow from the exertion. If you've ever tried to stop a kid from moving around you know what I mean.

Kids first

This program is designed to help kids improve their current attitude, energy level, health, and provide a strong basis for success as adults. Whenever there is a decision about the direction of the program the first question should be: "Is this the best for the child?"

Fit kids have more fun

The exertion from fitness (even when the exercise is gentle) energizes kids and adults and makes them more positive. Fun just happens when kids engage in these activities.

Fit kids are more responsible kids

As kids make a contract with parents, teachers, leaders or themselves, they start the process of being responsible people.

Fit kids eat good-tasting energizing food

In this book you'll find a variety of foods, menu choices, snacks, and other suggestions from highly acclaimed dietician Nancy Clark.

Positive reinforcement gets results

Recognizing kids for their efforts and accomplishments tells them that they are successful. Kids tend to do activities where they can succeed. Parents and teachers can make this happen every day.

Fit kids are smarter kids

Any kid who wants to pursue the limitless benefits of fitness has to be a smart kid, but there's much more to this story. Read on!

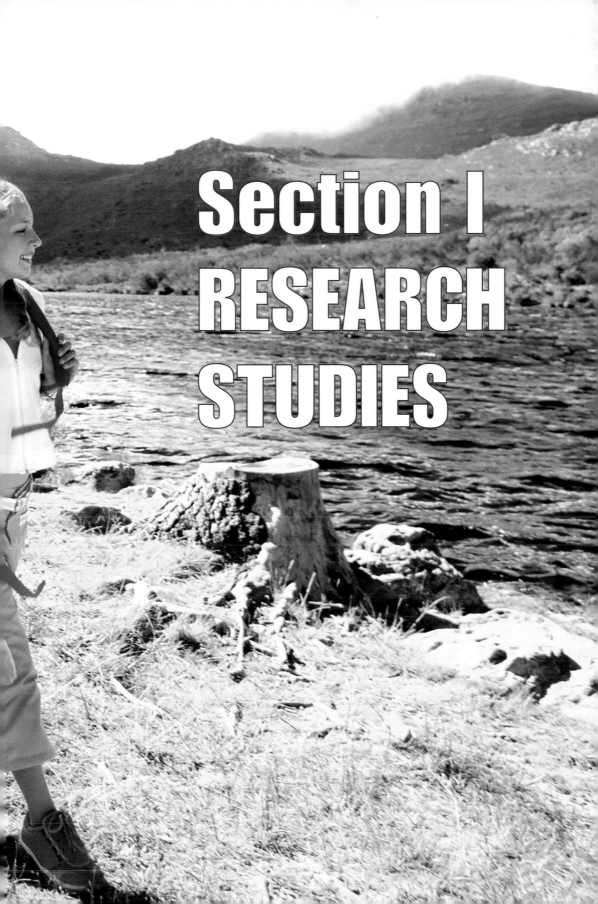

Section I
RESEARCH
STUDIES

The Connection Between Fitness and Smartness

After reading the studies in this book on the researched benefits of exercise, many sedentary citizens have become smart by rising off the couch and exercising. Smart parents have introduced their kids to the joy of exercise because they want to help their children prepare for life in the best way, while having productive fun. The evidence is overwhelming that a few minutes of exercise each day will make one feel better, think better, enjoy life more, perform better, and very possibly help you earn more money. Listed below are a number of studies that show how exercise promotes a continual series of behavioral changes that help kids be more successful in school and in life.

It is clear that our kids are getting fatter in dramatic numbers. The research listed in the next chapter shows that obese kids don't do as well in school, become obese adults, earn less money, and dramatically increase the health care costs for all of us. Exercise and healthy eating can give kids and adults control over obesity. For most citizens, the choice is simple: insert minimal exercise into your day, and eat healthier food, or get fatter and experience more health problems each year.

Note: A bibliography can be found at the end of this chapter

Increased physical activity leads to higher academic achievement

- Better test scores, when physical activity is increased, Shephard, R.J., 1997.
- Math scores are better when physical activity is increased, Shephard et al, 1994; Thomas et al, 1994
- Math scores improved when physical activity was increased, Dwyer et al, 1983.
- GPA and attendance improved when physical activity was increased, Collingwood, 2000.
- More strenuous physical activity results in the following: better academic achievement, better math scores, improved reading and writing scores, and a reduction in disruptive behavior. Symons et al, 1997.

- Exercise results in better brain activity, while it improves functioning in parts of the brain, and helps to make better connections between neurons, Boyd et al, 1997.
- Increased blood flow to the brain. Moderate to high intensity exercise promotes a significant increase in cerebral blood flow. Jorgensen et al.
- Cognitive functioning helped by exercise Etnier, 1997.
- Higher physical fitness levels in 5th, 7th, and 9th grade students are associated with higher academic achievement. California Dept of Education ongoing program with over 1 million kids annually enrolled. NASPE, 2005, Calif Dept of Ed, 2005.
- Teachers: Improved student attentiveness, and more: De Mondenard, JP, 1989
  -improved concentration
  -improved academic performance
  -children calmer in class and more energetic when studying
  -physical activity positively influences performance during the school day
- Parent observations: Improved interest in school, plus... De Mondenard, JP, 1989
  -greater concentration,
  -improved scholastic performance

Self esteem, depression, physical activity and academic achievement

- Self-esteem increased with athletic participation and was related to academic performance, motivation and mood, Boyd et al (1997) and Harter (1999).
- Physical activity reduces depression and anxiety throughout a lifetime. Dunn et al
- An increase or introduction of physical activity was associated with higher self-reported GPA, self esteem, and higher self-reported and school admin reported academic performance and achievement. (Field, 2001; Dwyer 1996; Dwyer 2001; Linger 1999).
- Fit kids have more energy Schoenthaler, S, 1991 and ASFSA 1989.

Proper eating and academic performance

Don't assume that families with substantial incomes have kids that eat nutritious meals. All parents should monitor diet, and most parents who do so are surprised at nutritional deficiencies. Here are some of the facts:

* Nutritional deficiencies that are minimal without clinical signs affect intelligence and academic performance. Schoenthaler et al. 1991.
* Students with the lowest level of dietary protein score lower on achievement tests AFSFA 1989.
* Iron deficiency anemia produces irritability, fatigue, loss of concentration, reduced attention span, and significant reduction of resistance to infection Parker, L 1989.
* Eating little or no breakfast reduces cognitive performance— even among kids that are well-nourished. Pollitt et al, 1991.
* Even moderate under-consumption of nutrients can produce lasting effects on academic performance and cognitive development. Center on Hunger 1995.
* Malnutrition results in significantly lower levels on reading comprehension, arithmetic, and general knowledge. Alaimo et al, 2001.

Bibliography

Alaimo et al, 2001, Food insufficiency and American school-aged children's cognitive, academic, and psychosocial development. Pediatrics July 2001; 108 (1) : 44-53.

ASFSA 1989, Impact of hunger and malnutrition on student achievement. School Board Food Service Research Review 1989; (1, Spring) : 17-21.

Boyd et al, 1997, The effect of a physical activity intervention package on the self-esteem of preadolescent and adolescent females. Adolescence 1997; 32: 693-708.

California Dept of Education, 2005, California fitness testing 2002, www.cde.ca.gov/ta/pf/documents/govreport2005.pdf

Burrows et al, 2002, Possible risk factors in the development of eating disorders in overweight pre-adolescent girls. Int J Obes 2002; 26 : 1268-1273.

Center on Hunger, 1995, Statement on the Link between Nutrition and Cognitive Development in Children. Medford MA: Tufts Univ School of Nutrition 1995.

Collingwood 2000, Physical Training as a substance abuse prevention intervention for youth, J Drug Educ 2000, 30(4):435-451.

Datar et al, 2004, Childhood overweight and academic performance: national study of kindergartners and first graders. Obes Res 2004; 12 : 58-68.

De Mondenard, JP. Practice of sport improves intellectual performance: Physical exercise and study. A beneficial association, Medecine du Sport 63: 137-139, 1989.

Dwyer et al, 1983, An Investigation of the effects of daily physical activity on the health of primary students in South Australia, Int J Epidimol. 1983, 12:308-313.

Etnier et al, 1997, The influence of Physical fitness and exercise upon cognitive functioning: a META-ANALYSIS. J Sport Exerc Psychol, 1997; 19: 249-278.

Falkner et al, 2001, Social, educational, and psychological correlates of weight status in adolescents. Obes Res 2001; 9 : 32-42.

Harter, S. 1999, The construction of the self: a developmental perspective. 1999. New York: The Guilford Press.

Kimm et al, 1997, Self-esteem and adiposity in black and white girls: the HHLBI Growth and Health Study. Ann Epidemiol 1997; 7 : 550-560.

NASPE (Nat'l Assn for Sport & Physical Ed), 2005, New study proves physical fit kids perform better academically. www.aahperd.org/naspe/template.cfm?template = pr_121002.html

Parker, L, 1989, The relationship between nutrition and learning a school employees's guide to information and action. Washington National Education Assoc. 1989.

Pollitt et al, 1991, Brief fasting, stress, and cognition in children. American Journal of Clinical Nutrition 1991; 34 (Aug) : 1526-1533.

Shephard, R.J., Curricular PA and Academic Performance, Pediatric Exercise Science 1997; 9: 113-126.

Symons et al, 1997, Bridging student health risks and AA through comprehensive school health programs. Jour of Sch Health 1997; 67(6): 220-227.

Thomas et al, 1994, Exercise and cognitive function, in Bouchard & Stephens Physical activity, fitness and health International proceedings and consensus statement pp521-529, Human Kinetics.

Sigrid Quendler, The link between Nutrition, Physical Activity, and Academic Achievement 2005, Symposium on Physical Activity, Physical Fitness, and Academic Performance.

Symposium on Physical Activity, Physical fitness, and Academic Performance, March 23, 2005 thanks to Julie A. Gazmararian, MPH, PhD. Emory Center on Health Outcomes and Quality.

Research: The Serious Threat of Obesity

"Failing to reverse the trend in childhood obesity means that many obese children, over their lifetimes, could experience significant impairments in multiple domains of functioning. They are more likely to be chronically ill, to have a negative impact on their earning potential, and to even die prematurely." Preventing Childhood Obesity by the Institute of Medicine of the National Academies.

Note: A bibliography can be found at the end of this chapter

Obesity leads to reduced academic achievement, depression, etc.

Overweight and obese kids are at risk of poor test scores, being held back in school, low self esteem and depression. Falkner et al (2001), Datar et al (2004), Kimm et al (1997), and Burrows (2002).

Obesity reduces opportunity, income, chance of being married

Overweight women 16-24 years old who were overweight completed fewer years of school, earned less money, and were less likely to be married (Gortmaker et al, 1993).

Obese children are stigmatized...

...and subject to negative stereotyping and discrimination by their peers. Schwartz and Puhl, 2003; Strauss and Pollack, 2003).

Exercise/lifestyle trends promoting obesity:

- Children 8-18 years of age spend an average of 6 hours and 43 minutes a day using media (TV, computer, etc). Rideout et al 1999.
- The average parent today is twice as likely to be obese as 30 years ago while genetic susceptibility has not changed during this period.
- Children born to mothers who were obese at the time of conception were twice as likely to be obese at 4 years of age (Whitaker, 2004b)
- Inactivity as a child is linked to sedentary adulthood. COPEC/Van Mil et al
- Adult promotion and example shapes kids habits of physical activity: a study of identical twins www.webmd.com/content/Article/113/110760.htm
- The prevalence of childhood obesity has more than doubled for preschool children (ages 2-5) and more than tripled for children ages 6-11.
- Poor diet and physical inactivity will overtake smoking as the leading cause of US deaths and cost our society more than smoking (Keeler et al, 1989)
- An estimated 61.5% of children aged 9-13 years do not participate in any organized physical activity during non-school hours (CDC, 2003a)
- 22.6% of children don't engage in any free time physical activity (CDC, 2003a)
- 8.0% of elementary schools, 6.4% of middle schools, and 5.8% of high schools provided daily physical education for all students for the school year. (Burgeson et al, 2001)
- High School students in grades 9-12 are not engaging in recommended levels of physical activity (CDC, 2003b, 2004c)
- Daily enrollment in physical education classes declined among high school students from 42% in 1991 to 25% in 1995(DHHS, 1996)

- From 1977 to 2001, there was a marked decline in children's walking to school from 20.2% to 12.5% (Sturm, 2005b)
- Costs: "The growing obesity epidemic in children and in adults, affects not only the individual's physical and mental health but carries substantial direct and indirect costs for the nation's economy as discrimination, economic disenfranchisement, lost productivity, disability, morbidity, and premature death take their tolls." (Preventing Childhood Obesity, Institute of Medicine of the National Academy), (Seidell, 1998)

Diabetes a likely and costly outcome

- The increase in childhood obesity has resulted in an increase in Type 2 diabetes
- Those who develop diabetes early in life will incur costly healthcare responses earlier, increasing the chance of middle age blindness, kidney failure, amputation, cancer, and premature death. Burgeson et al, 2001 Physical Education and activity, Journal Sch Health 71(7):279-293.

Bibliography

CDC (Centers for Disease Control and Prevention) Physical activity levels among children aged 9-13 years—United States, 2002, MMWR 51 (33): 785-788.

CDC, National Center fore Health Statistics, 2003b. http://www.cdc.gov/hchs/data/hus/tables/2003/03hus059.pdf

CDC, 2004c, Youth Risk Behavior Surveillance—United States, 2003, MMWR 53(SS-2): 21-24.

COPEC Physical activity for Children NASPE 1998

GortMaker et al, Social and economic consequences of overweight in adolescence and young adulthood. N England J Med 329(14):1008-1012.

Keeler et al, 1989, The economic costs of a sedentary lifestyle, American J Public Health 79(8):975-981.

Rideout et al, Kids & Media @ the New Millennium, 1999, http://www.kff.org/content/1999/1535/KidsExecSum%20FINAL.pdf

Schwarz MW, Puhl R. 2003. Childhood obesity: A societal problem to solve. Obes Rev 4(1):57-71.

Seidell, JC 1998. Societal and personal costs of obesity. Exp Clin Endo Diabetes 106 (Suppl 2): 7-9.

Strauss RS, Pollack HA. 2001. Epidemic increase in childhood overweight, 1986-1998. J Am Med Assoc 286(22):2845-2848

2003 Social marginalization of overweight children. Arch Pediart Adolesc Med 157(8):746-752.

Sturm R. 2005a. Childhood obesity—What can we learn from existing data on societal trends Part 1 http://www.cdc.gov/pcd/issues/2005/jan/04_0038.htm

Van Mil et al, Physical Activity and the Prevention of Childhood Obesity, Jour Obesity /99, 23:S41-S44

Whitaker RC. 2004b. Predicting preschooler obesity at birth...Pediatrics 114(1):e29-e36.

Sigrid Quendler, The link between Nutrition, Physical Activity, and Academic Achievement 2005, Symposium on Physical Activity, Physical Fitness, and Academic Performance

Symposium on Physical Activity, Physical fitness, and Academic Performance, March 23, 2005 thanks to Julie A. Gazmararian, MPH, PhD. Emory Center on Health Outcomes and Quality.

Preventing Childhood Obesity by the Institute of Medicine of the National Academies.

Research and the Benefits of Exercise

"For every hour you exercise, you can expect to receive two hours added to your lifespan. Now that's a great return on investment."

The evidence is growing that exercise will bring quality to your life—and the life of your kids. It will also increase longevity and will not harm your joints—when done correctly. This chapter is your guide to the research, so that you can read the documents and decide for yourself. After extensive review, it's my opinion, and that of many medical experts, that most people will maintain their cardiovascular system better and suffer less joint damage by regularly and gently exercising. It is also clear that starting to exercise early can significantly increase the benefits.

There are some risks in competitive athletics. It is well known that football produces many injuries that can limit activity for the rest of one's life. The higher the level of contact in competitive sports, such as soccer and hockey, the greater the risk of career-ending injuries—for both sport and life in general. This book promotes activities that have little or no risk to joint health. Be aware that there are risks in many sports. Because there are many individual differences, you should find the medical experts in the areas that are important to you and your children, and stay in touch about any problems that come up.

Humans were designed for long distance running —and walking

In the Journal **Nature**, November 2004, Daniel Lieberman (Harvard), and Dennis Bramble (Univ. of Utah) state that fossil evidence shows that ancient man ran long distances. The research of these experts, and others, point to the ancient bio mechanisms of the ankle, Achilles, buttocks, and many other components which are running specific adaptations. It's natural to conclude that humans were "born to run," that covering long distances was a survival activity, and that body and mind are designed to adapt to gentle and regular walking/running creating a treasury of internal benefits to body and mind.

Exercise prolongs life

Burn more calories and live longer. Dr. Ralph Paffenbarger conducted a highly acclaimed and comprehensive study for the US Public Health Service, which began in the 1960s. Results have been published in the **Journal of the American Medical Association**, April 1995 (co-authored by Doctors Lee and Hsieh). The conclusion: as the amount of exercise increases, rates of death from all major causes are reduced. Those who exercise more can statistically predict that they will live longer than they would when sedentary or with minimal exertion. This extensive body of research has also shown as a rule, that the more calories burned, the greater the benefit.

Exercise reduced death rate in women. This was the conclusion by Lissner et al, in the *American Journal of Epidemiology* (Jan 1996), from an extensive study of Swedish women. The researchers also found that reducing physical activity increased risk of death. Sherman et al found that the most active women exercisers cut their death rate by one third (American Heart Journal, Nov 1994).

Breast cancer reduced in females who regularly exercised during the childbearing years. This was reported in the *Journal of the National Cancer Institute*. Since the pattern of exercise is usually established in childhood, don't you want your girls to get hooked on exercise?

Colon cancer and GI hemorrhage decreased by regular exercise. Several studies show a 30% reduction of colon cancer among regular exercisers. Gastrointestinal hemorrhage research is reported by Pahor et al (JAMA Aug 1994)

Better thinking. Those who regularly exercised performed better on tests of cognitive thinking. Pirduso (Physical Fitness, Aging, and Psychomotor Speed: a review in Journal of Gerontology 1980)

Less depression, better attitude: Eysenck et al (Adv Behav Res Ther 1982) found that active folks were more likely to be better adjusted compared with sedentary individuals. Folkins et al (American Journal of Psychology 1981) showed that exercise improves self-confidence and self-esteem. Weyerer et al reported that patients who exercised and were given counseling did better than with counseling alone (Sports Medicine, Feb 1994). Blumenthal et al (Journal of Gerontology 1989) found that exercise training reduces depression in healthy older men, and Martinsen et al (British Medical Journal 1985) found exercise very effective in populations with major depression. Camancho et al (American Journal of Epidemiology 1991) found that newcomers to exercise were at no greater risk for depression than those who had exercised regularly.

Joint Health

"Physical activity is important for building healthy bones."
Niams.nih.gov/hi/topics/osteoporosis/kidbones.htm

Regular joint loading in youth assists in the establishment and strengthening of the collagen network of articular cartilage and contributes to the prevention of osteoarthritis later in life.
Helminen et al; Journal of Bone and Mineral metabolism Vol 18 #5 Aug 2000 pp 245-257

Exercise was associated with a significant increase in bone mineral density and bone strength—10 year study: walking, jogging, running and rope skipping are best. Lloyd et al, Jour Pediatrics, June 2004, reported in kidshealth.org by Mary Gavin.

Childhood physical activity enhances immune system, improves bone density and development of motor skills. Bunker, Psychological-physiological contributions of physical activity and sports, President's Council Phy Fit & Spts Digest, Mar '98/Sothern et al, The health benefits of physical activity in children & adolescents, Eur Jour Pediatrics, '99 Vol 158: 271-274.

Running does not predispose joints to arthritis Dan Wnorowski, MD, has written a paper which reviews research on the effects of running and joint health. He believes that the "majority of the relevant literature during the past decade" on this topic finds little or no basis that running increases arthritis risk. Wnorowski goes on to say that a recent MRI study indicates that the prevalence of knee meniscus abnormalities in asymptomatic marathon runners is no different than sedentary controls.

- "Studies have shown that joint nourishment is entirely based upon keeping joints in motion."
  Charles Jung, MD from Group Health Cooperative website.

- "We don't see marathon runners having more joint injuries than sedentary folks. Simply put, active people have less joint injury."
  P.Z. Pearce, MD from Group Health Cooperative website.

- "Running offers up to 12 year's protection from onset of osteoarthritis." BBC website 16 Oct 2002

- "Painless running or other activities which are aerobic and make you fit, help keep you vigorous for longer." Professor Jim Fries, Stanford University (commenting upon results of his research at Stanford on aging exercisers).

- "Inactivity was once thought to prevent arthritis and protect fragile arthritic joints from further damage. More recent research has demonstrated the opposite." Benjamin Ebert, MD, PH.D. as quoted in Dr. Larry Smith's website.

- "The notion that sports and recreational activities cause an inevitable wear on the joints just does not hold up when the scientific studies are evaluated. Few competitive or recreational long distance runners suffer severe joint injuries and many regular runners can recall how long and how often they have run." Ross Hauser, M.D, and Marion Hauser M.S.R.D. as quoted in Dr. Larry Smith's website.

Older runners reported pain and disability only 25% as often as those who didn't run. A study conduced by Fries, et al.

"Running or jogging does not increase the risk of osteoarthritis even though traditionally we thought it was a disease of wear and tear." Dr. Fries, from his study.

"Reasonably long-duration, high mileage running need not be associated with premature degenerative joint disease of the lower extremities." Panush et al, "Is Running Associated with Degenerative Joint Disease?" JAMA 1986. Subjects were at least 50 years old, mean # of years running: 12, mean weekly mileage 28.

No increase in degenerative joint disease in runners. "Competitive sports increase joint risk—but running risk is low". Lane, et al, "Risk of Osteoarthritis (OA) With Running and Aging: Five Year

Longitudinal Study". Studied runners 50-72 years old. Findings were similar to the conclusions of a study in 1989.

"Running seems to be devoid of adverse effects leading to knee degeneration, compared with other sports." Kujala et al, "Knee Osteoarthritis in Former Runners, Soccer Players, Weight Lifters, and Shooters" (Arthritis & Rheumatism, 1995)

"Runners averaging 66 years of age have not experienced accelerated development of radiographic OA (Osteoarthritis) of the knee compared with non-runner controls." Lane et al, Journal of Rheumatology 1998.

"Older individuals with OA of the knees (not end stage) benefit from exercise." Ettinger et al, JAMA 1997.

"Little or no risk of OA with lifelong distance running." Konradsen et al, (AJSM 1990) studied a group that tends to abuse the orthopedic limits (former competitive runners) that ran 20-40 km per week for 40 years. Other interesting studies include Lane et al, JAMA 1989, Kujala et al, Arthritis & Rheumatism 1995.

Note: The American Heart Association has a wonderful document that details the varied and significant benefits from exercise, citing 107 research sources. You can search for this on the Internet under "AHA Medical/Scientific Statement".

"Kids who exercise regularly can gain major control over attitude, energy level, bone strength and health."

Section II
TAKING ACTION

Kids Want to Exercise—Let Them!

Kids naturally want to exercise. From a very early age, when feeling sleepy and lethargic, kids move around more in the crib, push more against the car seat restraints, jump out of their seats, and run down the hallway. You can see the joy in their faces as they exert themselves.

Compared with a kid who sits in a room, an exercising kid will learn volumes about the body, the environment, how to change attitude. Exertion forces the individual to solve more problems, which is a primary contributor to becoming smarter. Kids who exercise from an early age learn to intuitively solve problems of movement and exertion, creating a greater ease in movement. Early childhood movement activities have been shown to trigger learning capabilities in the brain (see "Early Childhood Fitness" chapter).

Smart doctors have known about the benefits of exercise for generations. Several have told me, in various ways, that if exercise were a controlled medication to increase energy for learning, it would be the most heavily prescribed on record because of the known benefits in practically every area of the body. Unlike drugs, there are no negative side effects to exercise that are not under one's control. Regular doses make one feel more alive and positive, help one deal with setbacks and depression, and blend the mind, body and spirit into a team for top performance in any area. Exercisers feel more alive and are capable of enjoying more of life while dealing directly with problems.

Kids do what we do

Sedentary parents tend to produce kids that don't exercise. But an adult leader, who regularly exercises, is a major positive influence on the lifetime health of these future adults.

Kids often limit their exercise because we discourage them from doing so. So many schools limit the natural opportunities of children to exert themselves during recess, etc, and actually teach them to be sedentary.

Safety and liability must be considered—but many of the constraints imposed by institutions are designed to promote the convenience of the supervisors. Many rules have little connection with common sense. Surely there are safety issues and times when we should tell kids "don't move." But if this is a way of life, kids will learn to be sedentary.

Institutional control. When a child takes off and runs down the hall we scold them and often punish them. The "good" child is the child that is sitting in place, not moving, and not learning anything but how to be sedentary and to do what one is told. I'm not encouraging childhood anarchy. It is possible to allow kids to be active without disturbing everyone nearby, and you'll find the activities in this book.

There's no greater gift you can give a child than the gift of exercise. It improves stamina and develops the capacity to do more of everything without hitting a physical wall. Will power and mental endurance improve at the same time, preparing the child to tap into the capability of the total human organism. Kids can see that "work pays off" when they exercise regularly, which is a wonderful life lesson in itself. We want our kids to live a long life, and you'll see studies listed in this book which show this. More important is the fact that a kid who enjoys exercise will have a gift that keeps on giving, improving the quality of everything they do—of life itself.

The plan

In this book you'll find a strategy for making exercise fun, for bringing parents and kids together to exercise, and strategic plans to keep exercise interesting. Nothing is set in stone. As you try different activities, you'll expand the variety to keep it interesting. Kids can be fit at any age.

Running and walking are the basic exercises in this book, because they are the easiest to do, and provide the most time-efficient benefit. Other exercises are always encouraged, and a point system is provided to rate the equivalent efforts in the "reward points" section of this book.

Setting Up a Kids' Fitness Club in Your Area

There are a number of successful programs that are licensed or franchised. Look at the section in this book on these programs, and get in touch with the folks. Local YMCAs, recreation clubs and centers, even health clubs have sponsored kids' fitness groups. Here are some general suggestions:

- Get a group of parents together: When parents get involved by helping to get a program started, most become more committed to the program. Keep a file of interested parents and get them involved.
- Facility: Ask your schools, recreation center, or city park department. You may need to have a sponsor who works for these organizations.
- Promotion: Find a parent who can make flyers, distribute them, get free listings in the newspapers, etc.
- Entry form and waiver: See the sample noted below.

Parent/guardian permission

The following is a sample permission form, offered only as an example. Be sure to have your attorney look over and design a document for your needs. All organizations involved should approve the document, so that each is included in the waiver (when desired).

Permission form [supplied by Crim Youth Program]

I, parent/guardian, hereby give my approval and permission to the child (children) below to participate in the activities of the _____ (program). I know that participation in any recreational program may result in serious injuries to participants, and do hereby waive, release, absolve, indemnify and agree to defend and hold harmless the _____(organizing group), its director, staff, volunteers, organizers, sponsors, and other participants, including any other persons transporting myself or my child (children) to and from activities, for any claim arising out of an injury to my child (children) occasioned by their participation in the _____(program) activities. I also authorize the _____ (program) to utilize any photographs and videotapes of my child's (children's) and my participation in the _____ (program) for any and all purposes. By signing my name below I hereby certify that I have read all the terms and conditions of this release and do intend to be legally bound thereby.

Name of participant (s) _____ age _____

_____ age _____

_____ age _____

Address

_____

Email_____

City _____State _____ Zip_____

Phone_____Cell_____

Emergency Contacts

Name_____Phone_____Cell_____

Name_____Phone_____Cell_____

Medical Conditions: Yes/No Explain

Parent/Guardian Signature:
_____Date_____

How to get kids to sign up

Don't ever underestimate the power of a reward, like a T-shirt. By offering a meaningful reward to children, you can often get them to sign up. Once they meet friends in the group and enjoy the activities, most kids want to continue.

Motivational components:
- Weekly snacks for those who participate
- A medal or other reward at the completion of the program
- Trips to events
- Uniforms
- T-shirts
- Special discounts to local stores, etc.
- Keep telling the kids that they are athletes—that they are getting control over their attitude, fitness and energy

Teamwork Between Adult and Child —with Contracts

Example is the best teacher. A child who sees a parent exercise regularly and with enjoyment will often assume that exercise is a natural part of life. The teacher's lessons about the benefits of exercise have greatly increased impact when it is evident to the pupils that exercise is an important part of the teacher's lifestyle.

Contracts teach responsibility. When adults make a contract to exercise themselves, they teach the process of putting words into actions that can result in behavioral change. The success of any system is based upon each person knowing what is needed, listing the behaviors, and then following the list, every week. Contracts are simple tools that keep humans on track.

All training programs are held together by relationships. In order to communicate the roles and responsibilities of each, I've included contracts for each. Feel free to edit these to fit the needs of the individuals in your program.

Parents can make or break the best program

Once parents know the facts about the benefits of exercise, almost all will want to see the program succeed. The more parents who sign a contract to exercise, the more successful the program will be for kids. A short presentation at the beginning of the program, with a flyer about the benefits is usually sufficient. Early into the school year, however, it helps to have a "fun and commitment day" when there are fit activities for individuals and fun teams of kids and adults, with the presentation of the contracts.

Parent contract

1. I agree that fitness is good for my child—and that each needs to exercise.
2. I will schedule family events so that there is time to exercise.
3. I will support and reinforce my child's participation in this program.
4. I will show my support by exercising myself, at least 3 days a week.
5. I will try to get all members of the family to participate in becoming more fit.
6. I will help to make fitness a fun experience and a natural part of family life.
7. I will support choosing foods that are not high in fat or simple carbohydrates.
8. I will try my best to keep kids away from tobacco, alcohol, and drugs.
9. I hereby commit to do this for 6 months.

Parents Sign Here _____

Teachers and school administrators make a major impact on their kids

School systems are under pressure to show results. As you'll see in the research section, kids who exercise tend to learn better and tend to be more successful.

Getting the support of a school system, or at least the principal of a school, will increase the level of success of any program. I've also heard about a number of individual teachers who've made a major contribution to the fitness of their students because they did this independently.

The greatest level of success is usually achieved when teachers, parents, administrators and kids work as a team. When school administrators participate in some way in the fun activities, support is communicated.

The role of youth leaders

In some areas, the leadership for this program comes from a YMCA, Boys & Girls Club, Youth Soccer/Hockey league, etc. The board members of a YMCA, for example, will often have relationships with members of the School Board or area school administration. Key people at the top can open doors more quickly.

Even if the program involves one class at one school, the teacher and the parents should network with the sports teams/activity groups where the class members participate. Soccer leagues want and need to have a base fitness program for their players and in some cases could be the lead force for this program in a community.

Teacher/youth leader contract

1. I agree that fitness is good for the children—and that they need to exercise.
2. I know that it is important for the children to exercise regularly.
3. I will find time in the day and schedule exercise, at least 3 days every week.
4. I will show my support by exercising myself, at least 3 days a week.
5. I will strive to get 100% participation in this program.
6. I will try to make fitness a fun experience—and reinforce each child for doing it.
7. I will support choosing foods that are not high in fat or simple carbohydrates.
8. I will never use running as punishment.
9. I will try my best to keep kids away from tobacco, alcohol, and drugs.
10. I hereby commit to do this for 6 months.

Teacher/Youth Leader Sign Here _____

The child's contract

With the signing of the contract, each child learns the process of taking responsibility.

1. I agree that fitness will improve my energy, thinking, attitude, and health: I need to exercise every day.
2. I will participate willingly in fitness activities in school, with family, and with other groups.
3. I will support the participation of other kids in this program.
4. I will insert exercise into my free time activities at least 3 days a week.
5. I will try to get all members of the family to participate in becoming more fit.
6. I will help to make fitness a fun experience.
7. I will choose foods that are not high in fat or simple carbohydrates.
8. I will not use tobacco, alcohol, and drugs.
9. I hereby commit to do this for 6 months.

Each Child Signs Here _____

Teamwork.....works!

Getting kids involved in fitness, and helping them improve their lives is an energizing force. It will provide an energizing and motivating focus that brings together adults that have no other reasons to work together—into a solid team. This process of changing lives for the better is extremely rewarding.

Every season in pro or college sports, a group of individual superstars is defeated by a real team of less talented athletes who played together. By working together, the program gets more and more successful. When working as a team, everyone benefits—especially the kids.

Resources

The Center for Disease Control and Prevention is a primary force in the United States for promoting fitness. Here are some suggestions for parents, with other resources at
www.cdc.gov/nccdphp/dnpa/physical/recommendations/young.htm

- Set a positive example by leading an active lifestyle yourself and make physical activity part of your family's daily routine, such as designating time for family walks or playing active games together.

- Provide opportunities for children to be active by playing with them. Give them active toys and equipment, and take them to places where they can be active.

- Offer positive reinforcement for the physical activities in which your child participates and encourage them as they express interest in new activities.

- Make physical activity fun. Fun activities can be anything the child enjoys, either structured or non-structured. They may range from team sports, individual sports, and/or recreational activities such as walking, running, skating, bicycling, swimming, playground activities, and free-time play.

- Ensure that the activity is age appropriate and, to ensure safety, provide protective equipment such as helmets, wrist pads, and knee pads.

- Find a convenient place to be active regularly.

- Limit the time your children watch television or play video games to no more than two hours per day. Instead, encourage your children to find fun activities to do with family members or on their own that simply involve more activity (walking, playing chase, dancing).

Related resources

Links to non-Federal organizations are provided solely as a service to our users. Links do not constitute an endorsement of any organization by CDC or the Federal Government, and none should be inferred. The CDC is not responsible for the content of the individual organization Web pages found at this link.

Get moving...for health and the fun of it, Dietary Guidelines for Americans, USDAPDF file (PDF-288K).
This brochure will help you understand what physical activity can do for you, how much you need, and how to fit it into your busy lifestyle.

Healthy Youth! Physical Activity, CDC Division of Schools and Health.

For more information about physical activity visit the CDC, Physical Activity Web links.

For educational and interactive Web sites especially for children and teens, please visit the links below. These sites discuss the need to be active and offer ideas on how to get youth moving.

BAM! Body and Mind, CDC
BAM! Body and Mind Designed for kids 9–13 years old, BAM! Body and Mind gives them the information they need to make healthy lifestyle choices.

Powerful Bones. Powerful Girls.™
Educates and encourages girls aged 9-12 years to establish lifelong, healthy habits that build and maintain strong bones.

VERB™
It's What You do. Encouraging tweens to be physically active on a continued basis.

www.fitnessfinders.org

www.tbonerun.com: click "resources"

Being a Good Coach

When you teach a child how to enjoy exercise and help him/her make it a habit, you have given a gift that keeps on giving. An exercise session is a powerful tool to manage and improve attitude, motivation, energy, stress release, and long-term health. Helping people improve the quality of their lives will not only bestow a great deal of inner satisfaction: studies show a boost to the immune system.

Motivation to exercise increases when you serve as a role model. You'll also inspire yourself to learn more about fitness. Most adults who teach kids find that they study and learn the principles of training better as they explain them to others.

In this book, running and walking are used as example because they are the most time-efficient and convenient. If you are doing other exercises, just follow the guidelines of training and rest as presented.

Get them a good textbook—and a journal
My books *Getting started, Walking, & Galloway's book on Running 2nd Ed* are great guides. Go over a chapter at a time with your kids, starting at the beginning. Highlight the key passages in the book for

him or her. You don't have to do this on every chapter, but it really helps to get each novice headed in the right direction. Get the child a journal or notebook, and teach him/her how to use it. My *Training Journal* has been used by a lot of different programs.

Start with a little exercise, and gradually increase

When children are doing any new activity, or doing more than they have done in the recent past, don't let them exceed their limits during the first few days—about 5-10 minutes at first, and walk more frequently (if running is involved). Gradually increase the amount. At first, it is better to exercise every other day. Listen for huffing and puffing—a sure sign that the individual is pushing too hard.

Make each session enjoyable
—especially during the first month

If your coachee is huffing and puffing, slow the pace, walk more slowly, and make other adjustments from the beginning of every exercise session. If there is any sign of struggle, then stop for that day. Continue with gentle exercise if the novice recovers.

Low blood sugar

Before starting, if you suspect that your kid(s) are experiencing low blood sugar, have pieces of an energy bar and water, etc. about 30-45 minutes before the start. Have a reward after each session—especially a snack to reload composed of 80% carbohydrate and 20% protein. On some special occasions, however, it's OK to have a reward snack that may be a little more decadent than usual.

Find interesting areas where you can walk or run
—scenic areas, smooth trails

Convenient routes near school or home, will lead to more exercise sessions a year. But once a week or so, an excursion to an interesting area can be very rewarding. It's great to have variety, and you should give your coachee some choice.

On each exercise session, have a joke, a juicy story or a controversial issue

This will break the ice, inject some humor, and result in a positive bonding experience. With beginners (adults or kids) who are struggling with motivation, the humorous moments are often the key to their wanting to exercise the next time.

Don't push too hard, but encourage

One of the most difficult decisions in coaching is whether to push or back off—whether to use a pat on the back or a kick on the butt. In general, it is important that the person get out there and exercise regularly. When motivation is down, reduce the intensity to reduce discomfort. The ultimate success is realized when the new exerciser wants to do it.

Rewards work!

After a certain number of weeks, or after reaching a certain level of fitness, surprise with a reward. It doesn't have to be something expensive or exotic. The reward allows the new exerciser to focus on his or her progress, and feel the satisfaction when steady work pays off.

When your coachee is ready, find a fun event to attend.

Races are such positive experiences for new runners and walkers. Teachers can set up "success days" when beginners can become athletes. Participation and completion is the goal of these events— not competition. Just having a race date on a calendar will provide the beginner with an identity that will increase motivation.

Tell him or her about your mistakes

When you open up to your new exerciser with a personal story, the lessons become more powerful.

Don't over-sell exercise

The benefits are so powerful that almost everyone who stays with it for six months will continue. Teaching and learning by being active produces success. If your coachee is falling asleep during your one hour speech on the benefits of fitness, you know that you've stepped over the line.

Your greatest reward will be an independent fit kid

Take it as a real compliment that your coachee will need less and less of your guidance. This means that you were an excellent coach, and that he or she can find another person to coach, thereby enriching another life.

Section III
ACTIVITIES FOR PARENTS AND KIDS

Early Childhood Fitness— a Head Start in Learning

Many experts, such as Piaget, believe that early forward movement activities provide a crucial foundation for all learning. Parents can enhance their child's potential, physically and mentally, by getting down and playing. Not only will this establish a positive bond with him or her. Positive parental contact and play has been shown to be a factor in intelligence and early learning potential.

Don't underestimate the power of example. Parents who take kids in a jogging stroller on their walk or run, or who exercise on a treadmill beside the crib, play area (etc.) imprint the concept that exercise is a natural part of life. It doesn't hurt to explain to the kids, from an early age, how good you feel when you exercise, what the benefits are, how exercise is so important, etc. When they are in a stroller or play area next to the treadmill, you have a captive audience. This will quickly change, so take advantage of it.

- Remember that each child will develop various capabilities at different times.
- Don't think that your child is "behind," just because another child can perform tasks that seem to be more advanced.
- Children will not be able to move from one developmental level to another until they are ready.
- To see what is "normal," visit www.envisagedesign.com/ohbaby/develop.html or www.pbs.org/wholechild/abc/physical.html.
- Certain activities can help a child consolidate the development gains that the child is ready for.
- **Again, kids develop at different paces, and, if behind, catch up quickly when ready. If you feel your child is not progressing at the right rate, talk with your doctor.**
- Make sure that your play environment is safe for young children
- Verbally reinforce positive behaviors and be positive. This will tend to produce kids who do the same.

Ages 0-1 Years: The foundation for fitness and smartness

Anne Green Gilbert writes, "Movement is the key to learning! Movement and dance activities such as crawling, creeping, rolling, turning, walking, skipping, reaching, and swinging are essential for baby's brain development. These specific and intensive motor activities make full use of baby's complicated nervous system and follow a plan. The nervous system of each new human being must go through a series of developmental stages before the brain can operate at its full potential. Using her whole body, her movements, and all her senses, the baby "programs" her motor/perceptual equipment, her nerves, and brain cells.

"Babies need to be on their tummies in order to go through the fundamental patterns that wire the brain and lay the foundation for reading, writing, socialization and healthy behavior." Gilbert goes on to say that when prevented from going through the patterns, kids "may encounter problems in school with learning and behavior no matter how intelligent.

"The good news is that movement activities that take children back through these missed stages and fundamental patterns can often correct flaws in their perceptual process and enhance learning."

I suggest reading Ms Gilbert's "Suggestions For Babies From Birth To 12 Months," from New Beginnings, Vol 18 No 2, Mar Apr 2001 pp 44-46, from which the quotes in this section came.

Crawling is crucial for development during the first year

"As babies drag themselves across the floor or carpet, they are using movement as a way of life. This 'freedom' gives them the opportunity to:

- Learn about the coordination of body and limbs in preparation for creeping.
- Strengthen and develop overall muscle tone and in their arms and hands, legs and feet.
- Develop their hand, grasp, holding and letting go skills.

- Stimulate hundreds of touch and position messages that flow to the brain.
- Experience different textures and environment, which stimulate and enhance brain development.
- Develop visual skills e.g. a toy seen in the distance and moving towards it facilitates focusing at varying distances, called accommodation.
- Improve breathing."

This section quoted from the following website: www.gymbaroo.au/sections/publications/crawling_first.htm *by Daya Bhagwandas*

Crawlies.ca has a great page, listed below, on the benefits of crawling. There are many reasons why crawling unlocks the process by which a child becomes "smart": www.crawlies.ca/benefitsofcrawling.html

"Creeping (hands and knees) is the next level up the movement ladder:

- Improves balance and coordination.
- Helps in muscle development, especially of the hands, which is so important for the development of later fine motor skills, such as writing.
- Learning to coordinate the two sides of the body with the hand on one side and the knee of the other hitting the floor at exactly the same time, called cross movements.
- Improving body rhythm and timing important for thinking and moving, required later in math and writing skills.
- Appreciating the three-dimensional world from being on hands and knees, through the simultaneous development in vision, hearing and touch.
- Developing depth perception as the distance between the infant's eyes and floor when in this position, is the same distance between the eyes and book at school age.
- Improving accommodation as our infant is also focusing down at his hands and then up at distant objects, making many visual

adjustments from near to far and back again, as he will be required to do between blackboard and book at school!

- Improving the ability to localize and discriminate sounds near and far, all around him.
- Appreciating and learning about touch from greater freedom to explore.
- Developing the bone structures and muscle tone for upright position and walking.
- Making greater respiratory improvement for general health, vocalization (babbling) and talking.
- Will learn to sit independently.

"Let your infant sit and walk in his own time. It is important for parents to realize that infants will sit themselves when their back muscles are ready. In normal development, this occurs about the time of creeping - the infant pivots sideways and sits. Just provide the appropriate opportunities and allow nature to dictate the terms of development.

"There is a reason for each stage. Do not be in a hurry for your child to walk, for it is not how early he walks, but how much he learns about himself and his world before he walks that will influence the development of his intelligence."

The material from this section (including the bullets at the top) was derived from the work of Daya Bhagwandas, from the following webpage:
www.gymbaroo.au/sections/publications/crawling_first.htm.

Balance

"Balance develops from the time an infant first raises its head against the forces of gravity. As its brain puts together messages from the inner ear, the neck muscles and the eyes, the infant, with head raised and held steady, looks at the world. The vital building blocks of learning have begun.

"Even a seemingly small 'hiccup' in the area of balance can lead to immaturity in later skills and may even cause learning difficulties by school age.

"To help children develop balance, learn about activities which are not only fun, but also stimulate the inner ear, which has many connections to the area of brain which controls balance.

"Here are some great ways to provide joy to your little one at the same time help them in the attainment of balance.

- The old rocking cradle and rocking chair are comforting to the infant because they provide vestibular stimulation.
- Playing with your infant on large beach balls, rocking them back and forth on their backs and fronts.
- Swing your infant between two people in a blanket, toss them about 'gently'- they love it!
- Roll your toddler up in a blanket and then unroll him – leave his head so he can see, otherwise he may get frightened.
- Sing and bounce your infant and later rock your toddler on your knees to nursery rhymes.
- Dance, swing and jiggle your infant in your arms.
- Encourage all sorts of jumping and being frogs etc., as children get a little bigger.
- Young children love to skip – hopping first on one foot and then the other FAST. No one teaches them to do this - it is simply part of nature's plan.
- Walking along fence railings (a beam of large log will do) is a firm favorite. No one needs to encourage these youngsters, everyone wants to play this game."

The material from this section was derived from the work of Margaret Sasse, the director of Toddler Kindy GymbaROO – her latest book Tomorrow's Children is available from GymbaROO.

Ages 2 to 5

"What to Expect. During this time children master many basic movement skills, such as:

- catching
- rolling
- bouncing
- kicking and tossing a ball
- hitting a ball with a bat
- jumping
- hopping
- skipping
- running
- walking on a straight line or low balance beam
- doing a running jump
- pedaling a tricycle
- galloping
- chasing and being chased

"Children this age love to use their imagination.

"Parents need to foster social, intellectual and physical development during these "building block" years. The skills learned during this time lay a solid foundation for grasping more complicated sports and activities. Learning the basics will help your child experience success later on.

"Try taking your child to movement classes that encourage individual creativity and teach the child to control his or her body in space. At home, try telling imaginary stories about animals or storybook characters and let your child act out the stories. Emphasize movement as play, and be sure to encourage and praise your child's desire to explore movement."

From www.fitness4youonline.com/child_fitness.html By Lisa Drago
http://www.ideafit.com/articles/fitness_child.asp

Ages 5-7

Various combinations of these motions listed above can be arranged in games. Alternate between the various modes to develop a variety of capabilities.

Ages 7-10

Running and walking, or other sports, can become the major activities while still using a variety of the activities in the 3-5 year old section.

Another Resource which describes the various modes listed above, with coordinated strategies is *Active for Life* By Dr. Stephen Sanders, NAEYC Publications, 2002
Fitness Fun At Home

The best physical education curriculum I've seen is the EPEC, an exceptional long-term project out of Michigan under the leadership of Dr. Charles Kuntzleman, and the Governor's Council/Physical Fitness, Health & Sports. The K-5 segment has been finished.

Heartbeat

An excellent workbook, coloring book, puzzle book, and word game book—about fitness and health. This is an excellent activity workbook for kids in fourth grade or above, for rainy days, etc. For ordering or other information, contact *www.fitnessfinders.org*.

My Fit Body and *Color Me Red* are two coloring books for kids that reinforce healthy eating and exercise—with lots of interesting facts about fitness. These are also available through
www.fitnessfinders.com

www.cdc.gov/nccdphp/physical/recommendations/young.html has information and recommendations by the U.S. Centers for Disease Control and Prevention.

Lessons Using Running/Walking

Teachers and youth leaders have used components of the following to maximize exercise during a 30-60 minute period. Adult supervisors should strive to see no kids standing around for more than a few seconds (as in recording results). Each lesson has the following components:

1. Instead of doing the "pep talk" as they stand or sit, have the kids start walking in a small circle as you talk. The kids will continue to walk as you talk. Every minute of walking or running counts.
2. Thank the kids, in advance for showing good effort during this short period. The effort they put out today will pay off in many ways.
3. Announce the reward system that is being used, and/or recognize those who have achieved certain levels—see the reward chapter in this section of the book.
4. List the activities and any rules for that day.
5. You can adjust the amount of time spent in each of the activities. Individual activities might start at five to six minutes and could increase as you wish—gradually. You may split the individual time into two segments: one at the beginning and one at the end. On some days you may want to have just a team activity or just an individual activity. You are in charge of this—just organize ahead of time.
6. Each kid is responsible for continuously moving between group activities, doing the individual activity of the day.
7. Conduct the activities—NO STANDING AROUND—KEEP MOVING.
8. Record the results—if noting steps or minutes (should be done quickly—minimal time standing).
9. Finish with another walking circle with positive verbal reinforcement—for work that is well done.
10. Walking only is OK during the first few sessions. After that, tell the kids that you want them to try short segments of running with their walking—at least. These help everyone feel better afterward.

11. Positive verbal reinforcement is a very powerful way to motivate everyone—especially kids.
12. Encourage everyone to clap and cheer for everyone else. This builds teamwork, positive attitude, and makes every lesson upbeat and uplifting.
13. The "magic meter" time trial should be done on the same exact course. This becomes a very positive exercise by the end of the program. Almost every child improves significantly.

Lesson 1

Pep talk

"Each of you is strengthening the heart, lungs, blood system. This will help you learn better, have more stamina to do other activities, and will improve health. This will also help you feel better as you go back to class, when at home, and when studying. When mind and body work together you can be the person you can be."

"Exercise requires you to work. Work is good for you and strengthens a lot of your hidden powers inside. You are starting a journey in this class to get better in many ways. I salute your efforts".

Kids, each of us can gain control over our energy and attitude through exercise—let's do it!

Individual activity Walk to a certain landmark, then walk to another landmark, and then walk back to start—repeat. After the first two landmarks, allow the kids to run that want to run. Traffic pattern should be arranged so that there is not congestion or contact. If using step counters, take a count at the end of 12 minutes. If not using step counters, get each child to note how many "laps" they covered, in 12 minutes. Be sure to count the fraction of a lap at the end. Write down the amounts, and store away.

Group activity "Success Check" If you don't have a track, measure 400 meters. It may take several loops around a small field to do this. Explain to the kids that you want them to run and walk and then listen to the time as it is called out at the end of the 400 meters. Walk the course with the kids. After the finish line, each child stays in line, and remembers the time—as they keep walking. NO STOPPING! Walk alongside each and record the time for each. Run exactly the same course on all three "Success Check" timings. In other words, if you did not measure correctly at first, don't change the course for the next two.

Finish circle—as the kids continue walking slowly
Commend all of the kids for their efforts on the "Success Check." Tell them they will have several opportunities to improve this time—which gives feedback on fitness improvement. We must keep walking after any exercise session, for several minutes. The muscles help to push blood back to the heart.

"Most of you have done a great job today. Each step can improve your attitude, and the good feelings you get from having exercised. Give yourself a cheer!"

Lesson 2

Pep talk
Getting smarter
"A growing number of studies show how exercise improves the ability to adapt and better cope with the challenges of life. This is the essence of becoming smart."

Pushing back your physical capacity for life
Being fit at an early age gives one a head start on health and stamina. Exercising kids have more vitality, but they also tend to be more composed. Why is this? Exercisers maintain a positive mental state. By injecting themselves with endorphins, they are more relaxed and confident. As you use the muscles regularly and infuse them with oxygen, you will feel better about yourself and have a healthy glow afterward.

Respect for one another is generated when you exercise together. When you cheer for another person, look him or her in the eye and say something positive.

Drug-Free: Fit kids find that they have the inner strength to avoid these substances that can ruin your life.

Kids, each of us can gain control over our energy and attitude through exercise—let's do it!

Individual activity: Run to a landmark, pick up a popsicle stick (etc.) and walk back. Repeat continuously. Count the number of popsicle sticks at the end.

Group activity: Indian running (see p. 68)

Finish circle (while kids are walking): Mention how great you can feel if you walk after dinner. Ask the kids to come up with other exercise options at home, with family. Popsicle sticks can be counted during this time. Give everyone a cheer for good effort today!

Lesson 3

Pep talk
The "exercise boost"

"The most common post-exercise reward is a feeling of relaxation and enhanced well being, with increased confidence. Once you get used to this reward package, it becomes an important and powerful boost to your day. Don't be discouraged if you don't get the boost every day. While a few tap into the good feelings from the first day, most experience peaks and valleys before the rewards become consistent. This is usually due to pushing harder than you should have, and over-using the muscles. It will be natural that some of you enjoy exercise more than others. If you start a little easier, and don't push too hard, your patience will pay off. It is better exercise too easily at first. By building your base of conditioning and by fine-tuning a few elements, you can help yourself enjoy almost every exercise session, almost every day."

Kids, each of us can gain control over our energy and our attitude through exercise—let's do it!

Individual activity: See how many steps you can accumulate during this segment.

Group activity: Scavenger run (see activities at the end of this chapter)

Finish circle (as they are continuing to walk): Ask the kids how they feel now, compared with how they felt at the end of the first two sessions. Commend them for sticking with the program, doing exercise at home, and making progress. Everyone cheers for a great effort today!

Lesson 4

Pep talk
Endorphins
"These exercise-induced hormones are natural pain killers. But they have a positive psychological effect that can last for hours after exercise. When you start exercising, internal monitors sense there will be pain, and initiate endorphin production to manage it. Many of the good, relaxing, positive attitude effects of an exercise session come from the endorphins."

Vitality
After exercise, you should feel energized, with the motivation and the awareness to cope with the challenges of the day. You'll also have a good attitude to enjoy your free time. When you are exercising within your current ability, you feel more alive, better than normal, for several hours—if not all day. If you don't feel this way you need to make some corrections—usually in reducing the exertion level (or diet changes mentioned in later chapters)."

Kids, each of us can gain control over our energy and our attitude through exercise—let's do it!

Individual activity: Create an outside lane around the recreation field. When kids aren't doing the group activity, they are adding steps and laps to their reward totals. Keep moving!

Group activity: Endless relay

Finish circle—Mention how pleased you are to see almost every person moving for almost the entire time of the period. Every additional step means more calories burned, and the "exercise afterglow" is extended. Let's have a cheer for the great effort today!

Lesson 5

Pep talk:
Pacing
Explain how fast runners win races by running a bit slower at the beginning of a race. "The best way to run any distance is to go a bit more slowly at first. Whatever you save in the beginning, you can use later."

Creativity
Teachers have told me that on many days, their kids show the greatest creativity when they return from recess or a Physical Education period. Exercise stimulates activity in the creative center of the brain—the right side. This is also a primary source of intuitive and guttural activity. Teachers also find that many kids find solutions to problems after exercise. While physical and intellectual resources may be limited at times (often due to stress), the creativity of the right side of the brain is boundless.

Your intuition or gut instinct is engaged when you shift into the brain's right hemisphere. As kids and adults return to work or school from exercise, the increased right brain activity enhances subconscious judgment capabilities and other powers we don't usually use."

Kids, each of us can gain control over our energy and our attitude through exercise—let's do it!

Individual activity: Scavenger hunt. Have 4-5 stations around the playground. At each station is a cup with small bits of colored paper—a different color at each station. Have 5 hints where the cups are located on a blackboard or piece of paper that is posted. During the period, when not doing the group activity, the kids should be moving quickly between the stations, then coming back for another clue. Count the steps it would take to go to all of the stations and award reward points accordingly.

Group activity: Do the "Success Check" timed session, as in the first session. Warm up for this by jogging and walking over the 400 meter course. As a group, walk and run (at the choice of the individual) for another 400-800 meters. KEEP MOVING!

Finish circle— Commend all of the kids for their efforts on the "Success Check." Read out the times of the first week's test, and compare with this week so they can see progress. Ask them if they were slowing down at the finish—and how to better pace themselves. Tell them they will have at least another opportunity to improve this time.

Have each person, as they are walking, say one thing he or she is getting out of the exercise.

Cheer for one another—you did it!

Lesson 6

Pep talk
An attitude adjustment
"Exercise has been shown to be about the best way to improve attitude, naturally. After almost every exercise session, you can come away with a better attitude—if you pace yourself conservatively and don't go too far. When in doubt, go slower at the beginning and take more recovery breaks.

Achievement

Finishing an exercise session gives one a genuine sense of achievement. This is so simple but so satisfying, and was certainly passed on to us by our primitive ancestors, who ran and walked past barriers to the next homeland. We feel better about ourselves when we have exercised that day."

Kids, each of us can gain control over our energy and our attitude through exercise—let's do it!

Individual activity—Step day—count steps (find some creative ways) One suggestion is to have the kids count steps for one lap and write it on a piece of paper or blackboard. Then they must count the number of laps. At the end, you can give each child a piece of paper that lists the # of steps and the number of laps. Ask them to use math to compute steps for the day.

Group activity—Prediction event

Finish circle—as the kids continue to walk slowly for 5 minutes. Be sure to cheer one another on, during any exercise session. By being positive and by congratulating someone for positive behaviors, you will feel better and help the other person. Show your individual respect for a person by shaking hands with a firm handshake.

Now, let's have a big cheer for being successful today!

Lesson 7

Pep talk
More productivity, less fatigue

"When beginners start exercising, they expect to be more tired during the day. The vast majority, however, discover that the opposite is true. Exercising in the morning sets your mind and body for the day. You are energized, with a good attitude to deal with problems, and bounce back. Kids who vigorously exercise during recess or PE have increased energy for an hour or two. Exercise at the end of the day relieves stress, and can produce more enjoyment of the evening.

Friendships and bonding

For thousands of generations, humans have walked and exercised together. During the ancient journeys, experts believe that many positive team-building and caring traits were developed: sharing, trust, relying upon one another, and pulling one another through difficult times. These primitive instincts are revisited in almost any group exercise—at any age."

Kids, each of us can gain control over our energy and our attitude through exercise—let's do it!

Individual activity: How many steps can you accumulate today?

Group activity (pick one of the group activities from the list at the end of this chapter)

Finish circle—as the kids continue to walk slowly for 5 minutes Each of you has a chance to feel stronger as a person by exercising each day. In this way you gain control over your attitude, your energy level, your health and your calorie burning. You are becoming athletes—let's have a big cheer for improving ourselves through exercise!

Lesson 8

Pep talk
Setting a standard for yourself

Many of the adults who lead our country, who are extremely busy all day, have said that it was the habit of exercise as a child that set them up for achievement later. Admission directors from elite colleges have noted that endurance exercise experience is a big plus for candidates, because the following lessons are self-taught:

- Hard work pays off.
- You are pulling from resources that are inside you.
- You feel the confidence to grapple with a problem that did not seem solvable.
- You find that you have more creativity than you thought.
- You can keep going longer if you pace yourself.
- By exercising on a day you didn't want to—you develop inner self discipline.
- Sense of achievement and confidence must be earned—and will be earned through regular exercise.
- Each of us has much more strength than we give ourselves credit for.
- Once developed through regular fitness, these characteristics carry over to other areas of life.

Kids, each of us can gain control over our energy and our attitude through exercise—let's do it!

Individual activity: Pick a landmark on the field, and guess how many steps it will take to get there. Then walk to that landmark and compare. Then, pick a new landmark and guess how many steps it will take to run there. Do it and compare. Keep doing this until the signal to finish the individual activity.

Group activity (pick from one of the activities at the end of this chapter)

Finish circle—as the kids continue to walk slowly for 5 minutes
The studies show us that for every hour you exercise, you can extend your life by two hours. That's a great return on investment. Let's have a big cheer for our progress!

Lesson 9

Pep talk
A greater sense of personal freedom
"All of us need some time to ourselves. Kids and adults respond

better to the constant stress in their lives when they exercise. Even when exercising with others, if the activity is not too regimented, each of you can feel a positive sense of freedom that is not produced by other activities. During your exercise, you can strengthen positive things inside, rebound from stress, and have a positive time to yourself."

Kids, each of us can gain control over our energy and our attitude through exercise—let's do it!

Individual activity: Pick your own course and see how many steps you can accumulate in 15 minutes.

Group activity: (Pick one from the list at the end of this chapter)

Finish circle—as the kids continue to walk slowly for 5 minutes Each of you has a lot more inner strength inside than you realize. The gentle challenges of exercise help you to find the source of this. Let's cheer one another for a great workout today!

Lesson 10

Pep talk
"You are empowered"
"A primary mission of our exercise is to help you empower yourself to feel better through exercise. If the enjoyment is there, the pounds—and stress—can be burned off. Everyone knows that there will be motivational down times. Focus on the good mental feelings after exercise and you'll have a "carrot on a stick" to keep you going when you want to quit.

Exercise has been shown to increase the quality of life. When you get in shape, you feel more mentally alive, and have more vitality to do other things than you would. At one time, your exercise increases energy level, reduces disease risk, helps you think better, and allows for a great night's sleep."

Kids, each of us can gain control over our energy and our attitude through exercise—let's do it!

Individual activity: Walk to a certain landmark, then walk to another landmark, and then walk back to start—repeat. Traffic pattern should be arranged so that there is no congestion or contact. Running segments of 10-20 seconds or more can be inserted at the choice of the individual. If using step counters, take a count at the end of 12 minutes. If not using step counters, get each child to note how many "laps" he/she covered, in 12 minutes. Be sure to count the fraction of a lap at the end.

Group activity: Do the "Success Check" timed session, as in the first and third sessions. Warm up for this by jogging and walking over the 400 meter course. As a group, walk and run (at the choice of the individual) for another 400-800 meters afterward.

Finish circle—as the kids continue to walk slowly for 5 minutes. Commend all of the kids for their efforts on the "Success Check." Read out the times of the first week's and the fifth week's tests, so they can see progress. Ask them how they adjusted pace from the other two sessions.

"Let's cheer for one another—you are athletes! We are a team!"

Fit Activities that Are Fun

Scavenger run (From Crim Youth Program)
Form teams. Give each team a note that indicates a location. Teams must run as a group to that location to find another clue. Teams continue until they have visited all locations. The last stop could have directions to return some item to the captain.

Indian running
Divide into groups of 5-8 people. The pace should be slow enough so that the slowest in each group does not have to struggle to keep up. A walk break is taken after 1 min of running (a timekeeper

announces the walk break). At the start of each minute, the person in the back of the pack runs up to the front of the pack.

Continuous relay (3 person teams)
Use a track, or any loop that is available. You can use the outside of any field, playground, etc. If the field is not marked, place cones at the corners. Athletes must run around the cones. You may use batons, or just have the incoming athlete touch the next one on the team. If it is a small loop (less than 100 yards) the three person teams will rotate in succession at the end of each lap.

When using a loop that is more than 100 yards, the first person hands off halfway around the loop and stays there, waiting for the third person's handoff. The second athlete hands off to the third position at the start. Keep this continuous relay going for at least eight minutes. Gradually increase the number of minutes continuously running. No tabulation is made for first, second, etc. Every person gets great exercise as they continue to run throughout the term of the relay.

Prediction run
Using a blackboard, have each person guess the time each will run for a run of .5, .75, 1 mile, etc. Start everyone together and read out the times at the finish. Have each person record the time they actually ran, next to their estimate. Runners can run at any pace they wish—hard or easy. The winner is the one who runs the time closest to the prediction. Use this activity to talk about getting a sense of pacing.

What Is the Right Pace?

Young runners have a tendency to run too fast, especially at the beginning. In this chapter you'll discover how to set up a correct pace for each person, almost every day. It pays to explain to kids, the process of pacing, and how to use a watch to do this. Everyone should also slow down as the temperature increases.

The "Success Checks" are uplifting, as class members show progress. The adults' responsibility is to help kids keep track of the data, and explain the results. Everyone likes to see improvement, and these checks will document this positive process.

Note: My book Testing Yourself has training schedules for the 1 mile, 1.5 mile, 2 mile and 5K, with all of the drills and rest days built in. These are recommended for kids above the age of 13, who are motivated to improve further.

Guidelines for using the Success Checks:

- You are not injured. Don't do any faster running when injured. Make sure your kids know to check with you on this issue.
- The first one is run just slightly faster than an easy pace.
- Each successive one should be slightly faster than the previous one.
- Run with an even-paced effort, taking walk breaks as needed.
- The weather on goal race day is not adverse. Weather conditions that would slow you down include temperatures above 60F, strong headwinds, heavy rain or snow, etc.
- The adult will give a pep talk before each one. List the times that each child has run before—which is the current standard to beat.
- As the adult reads the time at the finish, each child must remember it and report it to the adult.
- After each test, have the kids walk in circles as you collect times for each.
- Congratulate the kids that improved—most of the kids, in most cases.

The "Success Check"

This 400 meter distance is our standard for children. This is one lap around a standard track, is easy to administer, and gives an accurate prediction for pacing.

1. Go to a track, or other accurately measured course.
2. Warm up by walking for 5 minutes, then running a minute and

walking a minute, then jogging an easy 400 meters (one lap around a track).

3. Do 3 or 4 gentle accelerations of 30-40 yards (no sprinting). Walk for 3-4 minutes.
4. Run the "Improvement Check": one lap around a track, using walk breaks as needed. Start your watch at the beginning and keep it running until the end of the lap.
5. On your first check, just run a little faster than a slow pace.
6. Warm down by reversing the warm-up.
7. A school track is the best venue.
8. On each successive check, adjust pace in order to run slightly faster than on the previous one.
9. Use the formula below to see what time is predicted during easy runs.

Before and after the success check, talk to the kids about pacing. If they are slowing down at the end, the pace at the start needs to be a bit slower. At the end of the program, the goal is to be huffing and puffing at the finish, while knowing that you could run a bit further at that pace if you had to. By the end of the program, most kids will find that they don't need many, if any, walk breaks during the 400— experiment and adjust. No sprinting (even at the end) and no puking.

Adjust for temperature. On really hot days, tell kids not to go all-out.

Galloway's prediction formulas
To predict a comfortable pace from the "Improvement Check": (1 lap around the track)

10 minutes of running or less: lap time multiplied by 1.5.
Example: A runner who runs a 400 in 2 minutes should run no faster than 3:00 per lap when running for 10 minutes at a time.

Between 11 and 20 minutes: lap time multiplied by 1.7
Example: A runner who runs a 400 in 2 minutes should run no faster than 3:24 per lap
Between 21 and 30 minutes: lap time multiplied by 2.0

Example: A runner who runs a 400 in 2 minutes should run no faster than 4:00 per lap

Recommended walk breaks by pace of each 400 meter

Walk breaks can be taken, from the beginning of any run, based upon 400 pace for that day:

Time of 400 meter	Walk break to be taken each lap on longer runs
1:30	10 sec walk after a lap of running
2:00	20 sec walk after a lap
2:30	45 sec walk after a lap
3:00	40 sec walk after half lap
3:30	60 sec walk after a half lap
4:00	60 sec walk after a quarter lap
4:30	90 sec walk after a quarter lap
5:00	2 min walk after a quarter lap
5:30	2 min 30 sec walk after a quarter lap

Examples:

A runner who runs a 2:00 on the "success check" 400 can run the following pace/walk ratio:
- When 9 minutes of running is assigned, run each lap no faster than 3 minutes, with a 40 sec walk break every half lap.
- When 19 minutes of running is assigned, run each lap no faster than 3:24, with a 60 second walk break every half lap.
- When 29 minutes of running is assigned, run each lap no faster than 4:00, with a 75 second walk break every half lap

1. This pace and ratio needs to be used from the beginning.
2. It helps to have group leaders who keep track of the time
3. Without group leaders, give each child his/her assignment written on paper
4. Remember to adjust for temperature
5. It helps to have parents to serve as group leaders who will organize a group and write down the times for each person in their group.

Reward Points

Positive reinforcement works. When kids know that they are working towards a reward structure, they can get through difficult days or workouts better. Many groups have used a point system to provide a basis for rewards. When you "ration" the time spent in desired sedentary activities, such as TV, video games, computer time, etc., kids will have an incentive to win points.

My wife, Barb, got hooked on running because her PE teacher used the Cooper aerobic point system. Points were given every day for the amount of time spent in a variety of activities. Each day, she and a friend tried to accumulate as many points as they could, based upon the activity. At the end of the week the points were tabulated and the high point leaders recognized. Barb discovered that running allowed her to accumulate more points in a relatively short time frame than any other activity. Here is a simple system that can be adapted to the situation.

Step Counters provide a good indicator of exertion. Each child gets a step counter at the beginning of the period, day, etc. At the end, the counters are collected and the totals written down.

Rewards: The kids who increase their points or steps are rewarded in the following ways:

1. Recognition
2. Awards at the end of the week/month
3. Certain levels of points allow more TV/computer/video time (example: 50 points = 10 min of video)

Point system

(Each minute of an activity gets the following points)

Running—5
Soccer (when running mostly)—4
Basketball (when running mostly)—4
Running with 1 minute walk breaks every 3 minutes—4
Rope Skipping—4
Running with 1 min walk breaks every 1-2 minutes—3.5
Walking—3
Cycling—3
Swimming—2.5
Soccer and Basketball when running half the time—2.5
Tennis—2 or 3
Hula Hooping—2 or 3
Skill Activities (such as throwing and catching)—1
If an activity is not on the list, make a judgment call as to how much exertion is required, based upon the points from the other activities listed.

A clock or watch is available at the exercise site. Kids are responsible for logging in the minutes, as they finish each activity, on a list posted near the watch. Teacher tabulates totals at the end of the period and records—or has the kids record for each on a chart.

Using a step counter simplifies the process: 20 steps = 1 point

Swimming is not a great fat-burning activity and therefore is not rated as high as other activities.

Fun Activities at Home

Exercise is a reward to the body and mind—energizing many systems at once. Adults can explain the many benefits as they get kids involved in activities that are fun. Before you get started playing, however, here are a few things to consider:

- Find the activities that your kids are interested in doing.
- Make it easy for kids to do the exercise.
- Be creative and adapt to new interests, and try short amounts of a several activities.
- Join in! When you do, even for a few minutes every 20 minutes, you'll tend to increase the quantity and quality of exercise. Remember that kids want to receive praise from you.
- Find a way to make every kid feel successful every day. Get every participant to yell encouragement to the others, with you as the head cheerleader. You should also verbally reward the kids that spend more energy than others and those who show a good attitude toward exercise, and those who give everything they have.
- Every minute of exercise is positive. Verbal rewards are much more powerful than you think. Keep telling the kids that they are getting into better shape, will feel better, have more energy, etc. If you have a reward system, as suggested in the previous chapter, remind them that they are earning points for rewards. As you mention the names of kids who are doing a good job, others will strive to improve to receive this reward.

Step counters or a clock

These are mentioned in the previous chapter. Have a shelf, drawer, etc. where the step counters are stored. An important learned behavior is that of returning the equipment after exercise.

The setting

Running and walking can be done down hallways, around the house, on porches, etc. Other activities can be done where you have room. Many teachers and parents have a carpeted activity room where they move the furniture for open space.

The "tool bag" exercise center

1. Collect a bag of exercise toys such as balls, hula hoops, racquets, etc., which will prompt the kids to move around. The bag allows you to quickly move to a park, a room, a lawn, etc., for some play time.

2. Spread out the tools. When you place the hula hoop in one corner, and a jump rope in another, you have established two exercise centers.

3. Have a snack reward afterward. As you enjoy the healthy snack of 100-200 calories, reinforce the habit of re-stocking the energy supplies with a snack within 30 minutes. This helps everyone feel better the next time that one exercises. Fat should be avoided in this snack.

Look at the "Lessons" chapter for other activity suggestions. Here are some that have been very motivating to kids through the years:

- A scavenger hunt. It helps to have a park, field or other open environment for this activity. Place little prizes (or pieces of different colored paper, and write down clues to the location of each station). You can have as many stations as you wish.

- A Triathlon. Set up a fun "event" in which the kids spend 5-10 min in each activity, and then rotate. This cuts down on boredom. You could run/walk around the block, then hula hoop for five minutes, then jump rope, do some sit-ups, and finish with a run/walk around the block. Secretly time each and record. When you do this later, tell each child how much he/she improved.

- Shop 'til you drop. Have a loop around the house, park, block, so that after completing each lap, the child would receive some play money. After 15-20 minutes of running/walking around the block, you will take a "shopping break." Kids then can spend their currency for fruit, little prizes, snacks or extra time in front of the computer or TV. You could conduct several segments if the kids liked this.

- Relays that keep going—see the lessons chapter.

The Galloway Run-Walk-Run Method

"By gradually introducing young muscles to running in segments, kids can experience the joy of running without significant aches and pains."

Walk before you get tired

Most of us, even when untrained, can walk for several miles before fatigue sets in, because walking is an activity that we are bio-engineered to do for hours. Running is more work, because you have to lift your body off the ground and then absorb the shock of the landing, over and over. This is why the continuous use of the running muscles will produce fatigue, aches, and pains much more quickly. If you walk before your running muscles start to get tired, you allow the muscle to recover instantly—increasing your capacity for exercise while reducing the chance of next-day soreness.

The "method" part involves having a strategy. By using a conservative ratio of running and walking, kids can gain control over the fatigue process. This is a strategy for life that will give young runners an easy entry into running, allow 30-year-olds to run faster in marathons, and keep 80-year-olds out on the roads, having fun.

"The run-walk method is very simple: you run for a short segment, take a walk break, and keep repeating this pattern."

Walk breaks....
- Give each kid control over how they will feel later.
- Erase fatigue.
- Push back your fatigue wall.
- Allow for endorphins to collect during each walk break—you feel good!
- Break up the distance into manageable units. ("one more minute")
- Speed up your recovery.
- Reduce the chance of aches, pains and injury.
- Allow you to feel good afterward—energized for the classroom.
- Give you all of the endurance of the distance of each session—without the pain.

A short and gentle walking stride

It's better to walk slowly, with a short stride. There has been some irritation of the shins, when runners or walkers maintain a stride that is too long. Relax and enjoy the walk.

No need to ever eliminate the walk breaks

Some beginners assume that they must work toward the day when they don't have to take any walk breaks at all. This is up to the individual, but is not recommended. Remember that each decides what ratio of run-walk-run to use. The best ratio is the one that allows each child to experience the joy that comes from running, and will vary from day to day.

How to keep track of the walk breaks

There are several watches which can be set to beep when it's time to walk, and then beep again when it's time to start up again. Check our website (www.jeffgalloway.com) or a good running store for advice in this area. Many teachers will mark places on the track for "walk zones."

How to use walk breaks

1. Start by running for 5-10 seconds, and walking 1-2 minutes (heavier folks should run less, walk more).
3. If you feel good during and after the run, continue with this ratio. If not, run less until you feel good.
4. After 2-3 sessions at the ratio, add 5-10 seconds of running, maintaining the same amount of walking.
5. When you can run for 30 seconds, gradually reduce the walking time to 30 seconds, every 3-6 sessions.
6. When 30 seconds/30 seconds feels too easy, gradually increase the running time, 5-10 sec every 3-6 sessions.
7. On any given day, when you need more walking, take it. Don't ever be afraid to drop back to make the run more fun, and less tiring.
8. When walking/running in groups, divide into groups based upon current fitness ability, using a different walk break ratio in each group.

Section IV
A GUIDEBOOK
FOR PARENTS,
TEACHERS,
YOUTH LEADERS

"The most important health asset you have is your daily exercise."

Why Exercise?

I believe that kids should understand that they were designed to exercise and feel better when they do it. Scientists who study the primitive beginnings of mankind tell us that before our primitive ancestors were clever enough to make tools and coordinate hunting strategies, they survived because they exercised all day long. Competing for a limited food supply in an increasingly arid climate, and lacking speed and strength, our forbears kept moving, collecting the "leftovers" that other animals had overlooked or left behind. In the process of pushing on to the next food supply, these primitive predecessors developed the muscle adaptations to cover long distances along with a variety of psychological and spiritual rewards from the exertion.

So, in the eyes of many experts, mankind evolved because he was an exercising animal—a long distance runner and walker. Other specialists in primitive man believe that many of the endearing human traits such as cooperation, mutual support and respect were developed while covering thousands of miles every year in small groups.

Getting smarter

A growing number of studies show how exercise improves the ability to adapt and better cope with the challenges of life. This is the essence of becoming smart.

Internal rewards

While the physical rewards described later are substantial, most long-time exercisers acknowledge that the psychological ones are even more powerful.

The "exercise boost"

The most common post exercise reward is a feeling of relaxation and enhanced well being, with increased confidence. Once you get used to this boost, exercise becomes an important component in your day.

Don't be discouraged if you don't get the "runner's high" every day. While a few tap into the good feelings from the first day, most experience many peaks and valleys before the rewards become consistent. This is usually due to pushing harder than you should have, and over-using the muscles. Some kids and adults enjoy exercise more than others. Keep fine-tuning the exertion level, be patient and observant. It is better to err on the side of making the exercise session too easy during the first few months. By building your base of conditioning, and by fine-tuning a few elements, you can help most kids (and yourself) enjoy almost every exercise session, almost every day.

Endorphins

These exercise-induced hormones are natural pain killers. But they have a positive psychological effect that can last for hours after exercise. When you start exercising, internal monitors sense there will be pain, and initiate endorphin production to manage it. Many of the good, relaxing, positive attitude effects of an exercise session come from these natural drugs…which are totally legal.

Vitality

After exercise, you should feel energized, with the motivation and the awareness to cope with the challenges of the day, or a good attitude that will help you enjoy your free time. When you and your kids are exercising within current capabilities, you feel more alive, better than normal, for several hours if not all day. If you don't feel this way, you need to make some corrections—usually by reducing the exertion level (or by diet changes mentioned in later chapters).

An attitude adjustment

Exercise has been shown to improve attitude, naturally. After almost every exercise session you can come away with a better attitude—if you pace yourself conservatively and don't go too far. When in doubt, go slower at the beginning and take more recovery breaks.

Achievement

The completion of almost any exercise gives one a genuine sense of achievement: inner satisfaction from hard work. Bottom line is that we feel better about ourselves when we have exercised that day. Adults can positively imprint these exercise enhancements by talking about them, and allowing each kid to say something positive about how they feel afterward.

Creativity

Teachers have told me that on many days, their kids show the greatest creativity when they return from recess or a Physical Education period. Exercise stimulates the activity of the creative center of the brain—the right side. This is also a primary source of intuitive and guttural activity. Teachers also find that many kids find solutions to problems after exercise. While physical and intellectual resources may be limited, the creativity of the right side of the brain is never ending.

Your intuition or gut instinct is engaged when you shift into the brain's right hemisphere. As kids and adults return to work or school from exercise, the increased right brain activity enhances subconscious judgment capabilities and other powers we don't usually use. Again, talk about this with the kids.

More productivity, less fatigue

When beginners start exercising they expect to be more tired during the day. The vast majority, however, experience the opposite. Exercising in the morning sets up your mind and body for the day. You are energized, with a good attitude to deal with problems, and bounce back. Kids who vigorously exercise during recess or PE have increased energy for an hour or two. Exercise at the end of the day relieves stress, and can produce more enjoyment of the evening. When adults talk to kids about this, a surprising amount of it sinks in.

Friendships and bonding

For thousands of generations, humans have walked, run, and exercised together. During the ancient journeys experts believe that many positive team-building and caring traits were developed: sharing trust, relying upon one another, and pulling one another through difficult times. These primitive instincts are revisited in almost any group exercise—at any age.

When you exercise with your child, you'll find yourself sharing feelings and emotions you wouldn't share when sitting down to a meal. The right brain, allows you to bond more closely even if you don't say a word. Communication is enhanced when you share the "after glow" of good feelings.

Pushing back your physical capacity for life

Being fit at an early age gives one a head start on health and stamina. Exercising kids have more vitality, but they also tend to be more composed. Why is this? Exercisers maintain a positive mental state. By injecting themselves with endorphins, an exercise athlete is more relaxed and confident. By using the muscles regularly and infusing them with oxygen, kids feel better about themselves and have a healthy glow about them.

Setting a standard for yourself

Many CEOs and other busy and famous people have told me that it was the habit of exercise as a child that set them up for achievement later. Admission directors from elite colleges have said that endurance exercise experience is a big plus for candidates. Regular exercisers learn that:

- Hard work pays off.
- You are pulling from resources that are inside you.
- You find yourself becoming more intuitive as the right brain kicks in.
- You feel the confidence to grapple with a problem that did not seem solvable.
- You find that you have more creativity than you thought.
- You can keep going longer if you pace yourself.
- By getting out there on a day you didn't want to—you develop inner self discipline.
- Sense of achievement and confidence must be earned—and exercise is one of the best ways to do this.
- Each of us has much more strength than we give ourselves credit for.
- Once developed, these characteristics carry over to other areas of life.

A greater sense of personal freedom

All of us need some time to ourselves. Kids respond better to the constant stress in their lives when they exercise. Even when exercising with others, if the activity is not too regimented, kids can feel more positive freedom than at most other times during the day. By conversing with kids about this, you can reinforce their understanding of this important benefit. They will be able to better deal with the stress from siblings, self-imposed expectations, puberty, dating, academics, marriage, job seeking, work, family, kids, aging, by having a place for their mind, body and spirit for restoration.

Tell the kids: "You are empowered"

A primary mission of this book is to help you empower the kids to feel better through exercise. If the enjoyment is there, the pounds, and stress, can be burned off. Everyone knows that there will be motivational down times. By reading these benefits, and talking about them, kids and adults are more likely to get out the door or on the treadmill. Focus on the good mental feelings after exercise and you'll have a "carrot on a stick" to keep you going when you want to quit.

Rewards

Kids and adults respond positively to rewards. Don't be afraid to use them as a psychological salve when overall motivation goes down on the hopefully few days when inertia seems overwhelmingly against you. These will be discussed later.

What Do You Need to Get Started?

Sure, there are "things" that can help you and make running easier: shoes, clothing, a training journal, watches, water belts, sun glasses, etc. Since I'm a running store owner, I'm very pleased that runners enjoy these items. But my advice to beginners is to test the waters gently, while focusing six months ahead. In other words, don't load up on everything you could possibly need for the rest of your exercise life—until you know you like it. Virtually everyone can feel great after and during a walk/run, etc., and that becomes a greater reward than anything you can buy for yourself.

One of the liberating aspects of running and walking is the minimal need for equipment. You can run from your house or office in most cases, using public streets or pedestrian walkways. You can use ordinary clothing and don't need to invest in expensive watches or exercise equipment, and you don't need to join a club. While running with another person can be motivating, you don't have to have a partner. Most runners run alone on most of their runs.

Medical check

Check with your doctor and your child's doctor before you start exercising. Just tell the doctor or head nurse that you plan to do the exercises that you plan to do with the idea of building up to about an hour, every other day. Almost every person will be given the green light. If your doc recommends against running, ask why. Since there are so few people who cannot run if they use a liberal walk break formula, I suggest that you get a second opinion if your doctor tells you not to run. Certainly, the tiny number of people who should not run have good reasons. But the best medical advisor is one who wants you to get physical activity, and wants to help you get out there walking and/or running because it is the most likely way that people will exercise.

Choosing a doctor

A growing number of family practice physicians are advocates for fitness. If your doctor is not very supportive, ask the nurses in the office if there is one who might be. The doctors who are physical fitness advocates are very often more positive and energetic.

The running grapevine can help

Ask the staff at local running stores, running club members, or long-term runners. They will usually know of several doctors in your town who runners see when they have a problem. Doctors tell me that compared with their other patients, runners tend to ask more questions, and want to keep themselves in good health. You want a doctor who will welcome this, and serve as your "health coach"; Someone who will work with you to avoid injury, sickness, and other health setbacks. Doctors have also told me that runners tend to have fewer bouts with sickness.

[sidebar end]

Shoes: the primary investment usually less than $100 and more than $65

Most runners decide, wisely, to spend a little time on the choice of a good running shoe. After all, shoes are the only real equipment needed. The right shoe can make running easier, and reduce blisters, foot fatigue and injuries.

Because there are so many different brands with many different models, shoe shopping can be confusing. The best advice....is to get the best advice. Going to a good running store, staffed by helpful and knowledgeable runners, can cut the time required and can usually lead you to a better shoe choice than you would find for yourself. The next section of this book will serve as a guide to getting the best shoe for you.

Step counter: An incentive for moving

There are many affordable step counters that attach to your belt or waistband.

Clothing: comfort above all

The "clothing thermometer" at the end of this book is a great guide for this area. In the summer, you want to wear light, cool clothing. During cold weather, layers are the best strategy. You don't have to have the latest techno-garments to run. On most days, an old pair of shorts and a T-shirt are fine. As you get into running, you will find various outfits that make you feel better and motivate you to get in your run even on bad weather days. It is also OK to give yourself a fashionable outfit as a "reward" for running regularly for several weeks.

A training journal

The journal is such an important component in running that I have written a chapter about it. By using it to plan ahead and then later, to review mistakes, you take a major degree of control over your running future. You'll find it reinforcing to write down what you did each day, and miss that reinforcement when you skip. Be sure to read the training journal chapter, and you too, can take control over your running future.

Where to run

The best place to start is in your neighborhood—especially if there are sidewalks. First priority is safety. Pick a course that is away from car traffic, and is in a safe area—where crime is unlikely. Variety can be very motivating.

Surface

With the correct amount of cushion, and the selection of the right shoes for you, pavement should not give extra shock to the legs or body. A smooth surface dirt or gravel path is a preferred surface. But beware of an uneven surface especially if you have weak ankles or foot problems.

Picking a running companion

Don't run with someone who is faster than you—unless they are fully comfortable slowing down to an easy pace—that is...comfortable for you. It is motivating to run with someone who will go slow enough so that you can talk. Share stories, jokes, problems if you wish, and you'll bond together in a very positive way. The friendships forged on runs can be the strongest and longest lasting—if you're not huffing and puffing (or puking) from trying to run at a pace that is too fast for you.

Rewards

You'll see in the section on "setting yourself up for running success" that rewards are important at all times. But they are crucial for most runners in the first 3-6 weeks. Be sensitive and provide rewards that will keep you motivated, and make the running experience a better one (more comfortable shoes, clothes, etc.).

Positive reinforcement works! Treating yourself to a smoothie after a run, taking a cool dip in a pool, going out to a special restaurant after a longer run—all of these can reinforce the good habit you are establishing. Of particular benefit is having a snack, within 30 minutes of the finish of a run, that has about 200-300 calories, containing 80% carbohydrate and 20% protein. The products Accelerade and Endurox R4 are already formulated with this ratio for your convenience, and make good rewards.

An appointment on the calendar

Write down each of your weekly runs, two weeks in advance, on your calendar. Sure you can change if you have to. But by getting the running slot secure you will be able to plan for your run, and make it happen. Pretend that this is an appointment with your boss, or your most important client, etc. Actually, you are your most important client!

Motivation to get out the door

There are two times when runners feel challenged to run: early in the morning and after work. In the motivation section there are rehearsals for each of these situations. You will find it much easier to be motivated once you experience a regular series of runs that make you feel good. Yes, when you run and walk at the right pace, with the right preparation, you feel better, can relate to others better, and have more energy to enjoy the rest of the day.

Treadmills are just as good as streets

More and more runners are using treadmills for at least half of their runs—particularly those who have small children. It is a fact that treadmills tend to tell you that you have gone further or faster than you really have (but usually are not off by more than 10%). But if you run on treadmill for the number of minutes assigned, at the effort level you are used to (no huffing and puffing), you will get close enough to the training effect you wish. To ensure that you have run enough miles, feel free to add 10% to your assigned mileage.

Usually no need to eat before the run

Most runners don't need to eat before runs that are less than six miles. The only exceptions are those with diabetes or severe blood sugar problems. Many runners feel better during a run when they have enjoyed a cup of coffee about an hour before the start. Caffeine engages the central nervous system, which gets all of the systems needed for exercise up and running to capacity, very quickly.

If your blood sugar is low, which often occurs in the afternoon, it helps to have a snack of about 100-200 calories, about 30 minutes before the run that is composed of 80% carbohydrate and 20% protein. The Accelerade product has been very successful.

A Trip to a Good Sports Store

"Good advice in shoe choice can mean the difference between happy feet and painful feet"

Most kids love to get new sport shoes, and are motivated to lace them up and exercise. A shoe store expedition is usually quite an event. There are so many lessons you can teach children when getting fitted for the right shoe. As you're driving to the store, and once you're there, explain the process and ask him or her for feedback.

1. The best advice is to get the best advice...when it comes to exercise shoes. Explain to your child that you've picked a store that has a reputation for spending time with each customer to

find a shoe that will best match the shape and function of the foot. Be prepared to spend at least 45 minutes in the store. Quality stores are often busy, and quality fitting takes time. Getting good advice can save your feet. Experienced shoe store staff can direct you toward shoes that give both a better fit and work better on the feet. A good lesson to children is that money saved on a bargain at the discount store is paid back in pain during exercise resulting loss of desire to exercise.

2. Tell the staff person which activities you will be doing.
Running shoes usually work better for walking. Side to side activities require a different type of shoe. The staff can help you.

3. Bring a worn pair of shoes. The pattern of wear on a well-used walking shoe offers dozens of clues to a good sports store staff person. Primarily, shoe wear reveals the way your foot rolls, which is the best indicator of how your foot functions. Shoes are made in categories, and each category is designed to support and enhance a type of pattern of the motion during exercise.

A knowledgeable shoe store staff person can usually notice how your foot functions

This is a skill gained through fitting thousands of feet, and from comparing notes with other staff members who are even more experienced (a daily practice in the better stores).

Give feedback

As you work with the person in the store you need to tell him/her how the shoe fits and feels. You want the shoe to protect your foot while usually allowing the foot to go through a natural running motion for you. Tell the staff person if there are pressure points or pains—or if it just doesn't feel right.

Reveal any injuries or foot problems

If you have had some joint issues (knee, hip, ankle) possibly caused by the motion of your foot called over pronation (see sidebar below), you may need a shoe that protects your foot from this

excess motion. Try several shoes in the "structure" category to see which seems to feel best—while helping to keep the pronation under control.

Don't try to fix your foot if it isn't broken

Even if your foot rolls excessively one way or the other, you don't necessarily need to get an over-controlling shoe—if you don't have aches, pains or foot problems. In this case, a shoe that is basically stable will usually work. The legs and feet make many adjustments and adaptations which keep many runners injury free—even when they have extreme motion.

Expensive shoes are often not the best for you

The most expensive shoes are usually not the best shoes for your feet. You cannot assume that high price will buy you extra protection or more miles. At the price of some of the shoes, you might expect that they would do the running for you. They won't.

Extra room for your toes

Your foot tends to swell during the day, so it's best to fit your shoes after noontime. Be sure to stand up in the shoe during the fitting process to measure how much extra room you have in the toe region of the shoe. Pay attention to the longest of your feet, and leave at least half an inch.

Size & width issues

- Running shoes tend to be 1.5 to 2 sizes smaller than street shoes: if you wear a street shoe size 10, you'll probably wear a running shoe in 11.5 or 12.
- Running shoes tend to be a bit wider than street shoes. Usually, the lacing can "snug up" the difference, if your foot is a bit narrower.
- The shoe shouldn't be laced too tight around your foot because the foot swells during running and walking. On hot days, the average runner will move up one-half shoe size.
- In general, running shoes are designed to handle a certain amount of "looseness." But if you are getting blisters when wearing a loose shoe, snug the laces.

- Several shoe companies have some shoes in widths

Shoes for girls and women

Women's shoes tend to be slightly narrower than those for men, and the heel is usually a bit smaller. The quality of the major running shoe brands is equal whether for men or women. But about 25% of women and girl runners have feet that can fit better into men's shoes. Usually the confusion comes in women who wear large sizes. The better running stores can help you make a choice in this area.

If the shoe color doesn't match your outfit, it's not the end of the world

I receive several emails every year about injuries that were produced by wearing the wrong shoe. Some of these are "fashion injuries" in which the runner picked a shoe because the color didn't match the outfit. Remember that there are no fashion police out there on the running trails.

Breaking in a new shoe

- Wear the new shoe around the house, for a few minutes each day for a week. If you stay on carpet, and the shoe doesn't fit correctly, you can exchange it at the store. But if you have put some wear on the shoe, dirt, etc., few stores will take it back.
- In most cases you will find that the shoe feels comfortable enough to run immediately. It is best to continue walking in the shoe, gradually allowing the foot to accommodate to the arch, the heel, the ankle pads, and to make other adjustments. If you run in the shoe too soon, blisters are often the result.
- If there are no rubbing issues on the foot when walking, you could walk in the new shoe for a gradually increasing amount for 2-4 days.
- On the first run, just run about half a mile in the shoe. Put on your old shoes and continue the run.
- On each successive run, increase the amount run in the new shoe for 3-4 runs. At this point, you will usually have the new shoe broken in.

How do you know when it's time to get a new shoe?

1. When you have been using a shoe for 3-4 weeks successfully, buy another pair of exactly the same model, make, size, etc. The reason for this: the shoe companies often make significant changes or discontinue shoe models (even successful ones) every 6-8 months.
3. Walk around the house in the new shoe for a few days.
4. After the shoe feels broken in, run the first half mile of one of your weekly runs in the new shoe, and then put on the shoe that is already broken in.
5. On the "shoe break-in" day, gradually run a little more in the new shoe. Continue to do this only one day a week.
6. Several weeks later you will notice that the new shoe offers more bounce than the old one.
7. When the old shoe doesn't offer the support you need, shift to the new pair.
8. Start breaking in a third pair.

Setting Yourself Up for Fitness Success

"As soon as you take responsibility for exercising three days a week, and making it fun, you're on your way to being fit."

You have a great deal of control over that part of life that revolves around exercise, if you choose to take charge. Adults who exercise, and schedule time for family exercise, are very likely to find that their kids exercise—as kids and as adults. The way you schedule your walks, runs (etc), your rewards, and fun events, can increase motivation. By pacing and walk breaks, you also can control how good you will feel during each run or walk and how quickly you will recover.

There is no need to ever experience pain—even when running. Adults may need to hold the kids back during the first three weeks.

The adult must take responsibility for keeping the pace slow with frequent walk breaks. Number one priority each day is to keep fun in the run—during each session.

- Regularity is important for the body and the mind. When you have three days of no exercise, you start to lose some of your conditioning and adaptations.
- It is fine to take a day off between exercise sessions. If you are running, the muscles used will rebuild and rebound more quickly and kids are more likely to be fired up to exercise. When exercising every day, alternate between longer sessions and easier (shorter) sessions.
- You don't have to use a running specialized training journal, like my *Training Journal*. A common notebook or calendar can work just as well to help you take control over your success. Schedule your exercise "appointments" as if they were your most important business client—or a meeting with your teacher, your boss, etc., and make sure that you show up at each appointment.

Top priority: Enjoying the first three weeks of regular exercise
A high percentage of kids who enjoy and feel successful during the first three weeks will identify themselves as successful exercisers.

Rules for the first 3 weeks
1. No huffing and puffing is allowed.
3. The short running segments should be very slow—followed by a lot of walking.
4. As much as possible, tell each child that finished the session, that he/she did a great job.

A special session each week...and each month
Kids look forward to special fitness events. Each week, try to have a different fun event, and each month something even more special. Teams and youth running groups often will have a monthly run in a park, followed by a picnic.

The Principles of Good Running/Walking Form

1. Upright posture
2. Light touch of the foot
3. Feet close to the ground—don't bounce
4. No knee lift—relatively short stride
5. Arms and shoulders should be relaxed—no excess swing

After having individually analyzed thousands of runners, in my running schools and weekend retreats, I've found that most are running very close to their ideal efficiency. Overall, try to run easier and smoother. The mistakes are seldom major. But a series of small ones can result in slower times, aches, pains and sometimes injuries. By making a few minor adjustments, most runners can feel better and run faster.

Inertia is our friend

Inertia is forward motion. The primary mission when running and walking is to keep moving. Very little strength is needed to run—even when running fast for short races. During the first 20 steps, you'll get your body into the motion and rhythm for your walk/run. After that, your goal is to maintain this momentum, while conserving energy.

Humans have many bio-mechanical adaptations working for them, which have been made more efficient over more than a million years of walking and running. The anatomical running efficiency of the human body originates in the ankle and achilles tendon. This is no average body part, however, but an extremely sophisticated system of levers, springs, balancing devices, and more. Our ancient ancestors had to walk and run thousands of miles a year to survive, and the ankle/achilles adapted to long trips on foot by evolving into a masterpiece of bio-engineering. With a little effort from the calf muscle, the ankle mechanism does a lot of work.

If you take short segments of running (5-10 seconds) followed by 1-2 minutes of walking, at the beginning of the program—most will experience no soreness, aches or pains. Even if you push too hard during the first few sessions, your legs should recover quickly if you back off to slower running afterward. But as you get in better and better shape, with improved endurance, you'll find yourself going farther and faster with little or no increased effort.

Other muscle groups offer support and help to fine-tune the process. When you feel aches and pains that might be due to the way you run, going back to the minimal use of the ankle and Achilles tendon can often leave you feeling smooth and efficient very quickly. This may also reduce or eliminate the source of pain.

How to go farther, with less effort:
- Shuffle—keep feet lower to the ground
- Shorten stride—reduces aggravation of tendons and muscles dramatically
- Touch lightly with the feet
- Quicken the turnover of feet and legs

Runners and walkers should avoid:
- Lengthening stride
- Bouncing off the ground
- Too much pounding on the feet
- Leaning forward

Relaxed muscles—especially at the end of the run
Overall, the running motion should feel smooth, and there should be no tension in your neck, back, shoulders or legs. You should never try to push through pain or run in an un-natural way. Even during the last half mile of a hard workout or race, try to maintain these three elements of good form, and you'll stay relaxed:

1. Upright posture

2. Feet low to the ground

3. Relaxed stride.

I. Posture

Good running posture is actually good body posture. The head is naturally balanced over the shoulders, which are aligned over the hips. As the foot comes underneath, when all of these elements are in balance, little energy is needed to prop up the body and keep it moving. By maintaining good form, you don't have to work harder to pull a wayward body back from a wobble or inefficient motion.

Forward lean—the most common mistake

The posture errors tend to be the result of a forward lean—especially when we are tired. The head wants to get to the finish as soon as possible, but the legs can't go any faster. A common tendency at the end of a speed session is to lean with the head. In races, this results in more than a few falls around the finish line. A forward lean will often concentrate fatigue, soreness and tightness in the lower back, or neck. Bio-mechanics experts note that a forward lean will reduce stride length, causing a slowdown or an increase in effort.

It all starts with the head. When the neck muscles are relaxed, the head can naturally seek an alignment that is balanced on the shoulders. If there is tension in the neck, or soreness afterward, the head is usually leaning too far forward. This triggers a more general upper body imbalance in which the head and chest are suspended slightly ahead of the hips and feet. Sometimes, headaches result from this postural problem. Ask a running companion to tell you if and when your head is too far forward, or leaning down. This usually occurs at the end of a tiring run. The ideal position of the head is mostly upright, with your eyes focused about 30-40 yards ahead of you.

Note: There are two strength exercises, mentioned in my books, which help maintain good posture: "arm running" and "the crunch."

Hips

The hips are the other major postural component that can easily get out of alignment. A runner with this problem, when observed from the side, will have the butt behind the rest of the body. When the pelvis area is shifted back, the legs are not allowed to go through their ideal range of motion, and the stride length is shortened. This produces a slower pace, even when spending significant effort. Many runners tend to hit harder on their heels when their hips are shifted back—but this is not always the case.

A backward lean is rare

It is rare for runners to lean back, but it happens. In my experience, this is usually due to a structural problem in the spine or hips. If you do this, and you're having pain in the neck, back or hips, you should see an orthopedist that specializes in the back. One symptom is excessive shoe wear on the back of the heel—but there are other reasons why you may show this kind of wear.

Posture correction: "Puppet on a string"

The best correction I've found to postural problems has been this mental image exercise: imagine that you are a puppet on a string. In other words, you're suspended from above like a puppet—from the head and each side of the shoulders. In this way, your head lines up above the shoulders, the hips come directly underneath, and the feet naturally touch lightly—directly underneath. It won't hurt anyone to do the "puppet" several times during a run.

It helps to combine this image with a deep breath. About every 4-5 minutes, as you start to run after a walk break for example, take a deep, lower lung breath, straighten up and say "I'm a puppet." Then imagine that you don't have to spend energy maintaining this upright posture, because the strings attached from above keep you on track. As you continue to do this, you reinforce good posture, and the behavior can become a good habit.

Upright posture not only allows you to stay relaxed, you will probably improve stride length. When you lean forward, you'll be cutting your stride to stay balanced. When you straighten up, you'll receive a stride bonus of an inch or so, without any increase in energy. Note: don't try to increase stride length. When it happens naturally, you won't feel it—you'll just run faster.

An oxygen dividend—and no more side pain!
Breathing improves when you straighten up. A leaning body can't get ideal use out of the lower lungs. This can cause side pain. When you run upright, the lower lungs can receive adequate air, maximize oxygen absorption, and reduce the chance of side pain.

II. Feet low to the ground

The most efficient stride is a shuffle—with feet right next to the ground. As long as you pick your foot up enough to avoid stumbling over a rock or uneven pavement, stay low to the ground. Most runners don't need to get more than one inch clearance—even when running fast. As you increase speed, and ankle action, you will come off the ground a bit more than this. Again, don't try to increase stride, let this happen naturally.

Your ankle combined with your Achilles tendon will act as a spring, moving you forward with each running or walking step. If you stay low to the ground, very little effort is required. Through this "shuffling" technique, running becomes almost automatic. When runners err on bounce, they try to push off too hard. This usually results in extra effort spent, lifting the body off the ground. You can think of this as energy wasted in the air—energy that could be used to run faster.

The other negative force that penalizes a higher bounce is gravity. The higher you rise, the harder you fall. Each additional bounce off the ground delivers a lot more impact on feet and legs. During speed sessions, races, and long runs, more bounce produces aches, pains and injuries.

The correction for too much bounce: Light touch

The ideal foot "touch" should be so light that you don't usually feel yourself pushing off or landing. This means that your foot stays low to the ground and goes though an efficient and natural motion. Instead of trying to overcome gravity, you get in synch with it. If your foot "slaps" when you run, you will definitely improve with a lighter touch.

Here's a "light touch drill": During the middle of a run, time yourself and/or your kids for 20 seconds. Focus on one item: touching so softly that you don't hear your feet. Earplugs are not allowed for this drill. Imagine that you are running on thin ice or through a bed of hot coals. Do several of these 20 second touches, becoming quieter and quieter. You should feel very little impact on your feet as you do this drill. This drill is particularly beneficial when you are tired.

III. Stride length

Studies have shown that as runners get faster, the stride length shortens. This clearly shows that the key to faster and more efficient running is increased cadence (quicker turnover) of feet and legs. A major cause of aches, pains and injuries is a stride length that is too long. When in doubt, it is always better to err on the side of having a shorter stride. The CD drill in this book can help you improve your turnover naturally and intuitively.

Runners will naturally experience a tightening of the running muscles. This is not usually a problem, only a reality. As the body adapts to the running motion, tightening of certain body mechanics are intuitively made to make running more efficient. Don't try to "stretch out" a muscle that is tired after a run. After-run stretching produces a lot of injuries.

Don't lift your knees!
Even most of the world-class distance runners don't have a high knee lift. When your knees are carried too high, you tend to over-use the quadriceps muscle (front of the thigh), resulting in a stride that is too long to be efficient. This often produces sore quads for the next day or two.

Don't kick out too far in front of you!
If you watch the natural movement of the leg, it will kick forward slightly as the foot gently moves forward in the running motion and then comes underneath to contact the ground. Let this be a natural motion that produces no tightness in the muscles behind the lower or upper leg.

Tightness or pain in the front of the shin, or behind the knee, or in the hamstring (back of the thigh) are signs that you are kicking too far forward, and reaching out too far. Correct this by staying low to the ground, shortening the stride, and lightly touching the ground.

Motivation and Mental Toughness

"Mental training gives you control over your attitude and improves motivation."

Left brain vs. right brain

The brain has two hemispheres that are separated and don't interconnect. The logical left brain does our business, school, and homework activities, trying to logically get to the bottom line. The left brain monitors stress, trying to steer us into pleasure and away from discomfort. The quiet, creative and intuitive right side is an unlimited source of solutions to problems, and can connect us to hidden strengths. When we learn how to tap into the right side, by walking and running within our capabilities, we will unlock powers that can be used in other areas of life, while we enjoy running.

As we accumulate stress, the left brain sends us a stream of messages during or just before exercise: "Slow down," "Stop," "This isn't your day," and even philosophical messages like, "Why are you doing this." We are all capable of staying on track, and even pushing to a higher level of performance—even when the left brain tells us these things.

The first step in taking command over motivation is to ignore the left brain unless there is a legitimate reason of health or safety (very rare), or, in fact, you are running a lot faster than you are ready to run. Here are three successful methods for dealing with the left brain, while letting the right brain solve problems and help you realize your potential. There is much more on this in my books **Getting Started, Galloway's Book on Running Second Edition, and A Year-Round Plan.**

Mental strength strategies:

1. Rehearsal: Whatever your problems, rehearse them before you start. Anticipate the negative messages of the left brain. Gain a positive vision of yourself making adjustments and feeling strong to the end.

2. Magic words: When you overcome a problem, attach a key word to it. My magic words are "Relax, Power, and Glide," because they refer to the positive side of repeated problems. Having now associated hundreds of successful experiences with the words, they can pull me through several miles of challenges.

3. Dirty tricks: These are funny thoughts and imagined actions that can get us down the road for another few hundred yards—usually to the end of your workout or race. One of my favorites is a giant invisible rubber band which I toss around the person ahead of me—to pull me along when I'm tired.

These allow the right side of the brain to work on solutions to current problems. By preparing mentally for the challenges you expect, you will empower the right brain to deal with the problems and to tap into the inner sources of strength: the essence of mental toughness. You're installing a software program that finds a way to get the job done.

Section V
NUTRITION &
FAT BURNING

Fueling Fit Kids

By Nancy Clark, MS, RD

Sports Nutritionist and Author of Nancy Clark's Sports Nutrition Guidebook

Well-fueled kids enjoy not only good health and high energy, they are also better learners for their teachers and coaches. Anyone who has tried to teach or coach hungry kids will tell you the effort seems futile! By encouraging children to eat the right foods and drink fluids at the right times, you'll not only help them establish good fueling practices that pave the way to the winner's circle if the child becomes more competitive, when older. Above all, good nutrition will enhance today's enjoyment of an active lifestyle.

As the parent, teacher or coach, you may wonder: Do young exercisers have special nutritional needs? In this chapter, we'll look at some of the nutrition concerns for growing school children, so you will know how to feed your active child for normal growth, development and high energy.

Day to day fueling for healthy kids

A good diet helps active children accomplish four big goals:

1 Grow and develop at the right pace.
2 Stay healthy, and if illness or injury does occur, heal as quickly as possible.
3 Delay fatigue and maintain a high energy level for exercise.
4 Enhance lifelong enjoyment of exercise and good health.

On a daily basis, the role of a parent is to feed the child a diet that supports those goals. This can be tricky, given our eat-on-the-run lifestyle that puts little value on home-cooked meals and organized snacks. Never-the-less, you can take family mealtimes seriously!

Kids who eat family meals tend to eat more nutritious foods while they benefit from the social interactions. Children who eat poorly are often the victims of parents who have failed to plan better choices. For example, if you are rushing off to work/school/practice and fail to pack some healthful snacks, the alternatives can too easily become candy bars or chips from the snack shack.

By pre-planning post-exercise recovery foods, you can have healthful snacks readily available when your child is ravenous. Take along a cooler with chocolate milk, juice boxes and water bottles, as well as bagels, bananas, and yogurt. This way, you can feed the hungry monsters, tame their appetites, and enable them to manage their hunger while you cook a wholesome meal when you get home,

Healthier, fast food options

If no dinner is planned, fast but fatty take-out meals can become an option that is "too-easy." If that's the case, here are some healthier options on the menu:

Burger King: Chicken Whopper (without mayo), Veggie Burger
McDonald's: McGrilled Chicken, Fruit 'n Yogurt Parfait, Egg McMuffin
Wendy's: Chili, baked potato (only a little topping), Frosty
Taco Bell: Burritos, soft tacos, gorditas, frajitas (w/o sour cream)
Papa Gino's: Spaghetti or penne with tomato sauce, bread sticks

In general, even when eating on the run, try to serve your child a variety of nutritious foods:

- Three types of food per meal:
  cereal + milk + banana
  bread + peanut butter + yogurt
  chicken + rice + peas
- Two kinds of food per snack:
  apple + lowfat cheese
  crackers + peanut butter

- Offer only small amounts of foods containing sugar (soft drinks, sports drinks, cookies, candy)
- Include healthful fats (nuts, peanut butter, olive oil for salads and sautéed vegetables) but sparingly offer fried foods (fried chicken fingers, french fries) and greasy foods (burgers, pepperoni).

Hungry kids need calories for energy

Active children may need as many calories as their parents—if not more. For example, the average active 10-year-old girl or boy burns about 2,000 to 2,200 calories per day. Among active six year olds, the average calorie intake is 1,600 to 1,800 calories. If your child is growing normally, she is probably getting what she needs. Her training will not stunt her growth as long she eats enough calories. If your child seems overly fatigued and lethargic, suspect inadequate calories.

Each meal and snack should provide calories from wholesome carbohydrates: grains, fruits and vegetables. These are the best source of muscle fuel for active children.

Grains

Grains include wheat, rice, corn and oats. Foods made from grains, such as cereals, breads, rice, pasta and noodles should be the foundation of each meal.

Ideally, at least half of grain foods should be whole grains, because they offer more fiber and nutrients. Some kid-friendly whole grains include:

> Breakfast: oatmeal, Wheaties, Cheerios, whole wheat bagels
> Lunch: oatmeal bread, whole wheat wraps, brown rice cakes
> Snacks: Triscuits (low fat), popcorn, toasted corn chips
> Dinner: corn, corn tortillas, brown rice

Despite popular belief, refined grains (white bread, white pasta) also contribute nutrients to a good diet because they are commonly enriched with B-vitamins and iron. Hence, if your child refuses to eat whole wheat breads and pastas, serving white breads and pasta can be acceptable, trusting the child consumes whole grains, such as popcorn or whole grain cereal, at other times.

Fruits and vegetables

Fruits and vegetables are Nature's vitamin pills; they provide the "spark plugs" needed for the child's engine to run smoothly and powerfully. Children should have at least 1.5 cups of fruits per day and 2.5 cups of vegetables.

This could be as simple as:
>Breakfast; orange juice, banana on cereal
>Lunch: baby carrots, raisins
>Snack: raw pepper strips, cherry tomatoes
>(with lowfat ranch dressing for a dip)
>Dinner: potato, green beans

Frozen, canned or dried fruit and vegetables are acceptable alternatives to fresh ones, and offer convenience as well as variety in all seasons.

Colors! When choosing fruits and vegetables, teach your child to eat a variety of colors: each color offers special health protective nutrients. The more variety of colors, the better. Examples of nature's rainbow of fruits and vegetables include:

Red:	cherries, tomatoes,
Blue:	blueberries
Purple:	plums, grapes, eggplant
Green:	kiwi, peppers, broccoli, peas
Orange:	oranges, acorn squash
White:	bananas, potato
Yellow:	pineapple, summer squash

Kids, fruits and vegetables

Fruits, vegetables and kids often seem like oil and water—they separate easily! Before you worry too much about nutritional deficiencies due to lack of fruits and vegetables, first closely observe what your child is actually consuming. Perhaps she is consuming these powerhouse choices:

- Orange juice.
  Just 8-ounces of orange juice provides the day's requirement for Vitamin C. Of all the juices, orange is among the best—and calcium-fortified juice is even better! To enhance consumption of OJ, limit the amount of other juices and soft drinks you buy.

- Colorful veggies: baby carrots, cherry tomatoes, pepper strips. When the before-dinner munchies hit, have a plate with raw veggies on the table, ready for snacking. Some kids like to dip the vegetables in lowfat ranch dressing.

- Tomato sauce, such as that used on pasta and pizza. This is a good source of beta-carotene (needed to make Vitamin A) as well as other phytochemicals and health-protective nutrients.

In general, you want to routinely offer nutrient-dense fruits— oranges, grapefruit, clementines, cantaloupe, watermelon, honeydew, bananas, kiwis and strawberries—and nutrient-dense vegetables—colorful ones, such as carrots, tomatoes, peppers, and broccoli. The good time to serve these is right before dinner, when the kids are hungriest.

Transforming the junk food junkie

Many kids eat a high fat "junk food" diet and seem to perform well. But the question arises: How much **better** could they be? My experience suggests even good athletes improve when they switch to fueling their bodies with premium nutrition. The right foods work better!

Perhaps your child can start viewing his body as a high performance race car and take interest in fueling it wisely with high-octane nutrition. He will notice the benefits in terms of enhanced performance. Balanced meals that have carbohydrates as their foundation (breakfast cereal with fruit, lunchtime sandwiches on hearty bread, spaghetti at dinner) provide quality calories, the "gas" that fuels the muscles with glycogen. Fruits, vegetables, dairy foods, lean meats and other protein-rich foods are also important. They are the "spark plugs" (vitamins, minerals, amino acids) that keep the body's engine running powerfully.

Although much of athletic success relates to genetics plus good coaching and dedicated training, proper fueling can make the difference between improving and dragging. Food is a powerful performance enhancer. If your child wants to train at his best—and compete at his best—he needs to include a good sports diet in his training program.

The following information highlights a few key points for fitness parents who want more details about how to fuel their young children appropriately. For complete information about planning healthful meals for your children, visit *www.MyPyramid.gov* or read Ellyn Satter's book, **Secrets of Feeding a Healthy Family**.

Pre-exercise and pre-event eating for energy

Fueling the body properly before exercise is very important for active children. Kids who run out of energy won't have much fun and may drop out of exercise and sports because they feel too tired. Some simple pre-exercise snack ideas include the following:

• yogurt with berries
• cereal with milk
• half-bagel with peanut butter
• banana and granola bar
• orange juice and crackers
• animal crackers and grapes
• other carbohydrate-based foods that settle well and are easy to digest. Experiment with different choices to determine which foods are most popular.

The night before an event or hard workout, your child can certainly benefit from a carbohydrate-rich meal. Spaghetti is always a popular choice, but any meal based on rice, potatoes, breads, noodles, vegetables and fruit will fuel the muscles. These carbohydrate-rich foods get stored in the muscles as muscle glycogen and provide the energy your child needs for stamina and endurance. When you talk about the need to "fuel up" at pre-event dinners, you teach the messages:

- Carbs, such as pasta, best fuel the muscles.
- What an athlete eats before an event can affect how well the athlete performs.
- Athletes should be as responsible with fueling as they are with training.

Note: You shouldn't serve a carb-based meal only the night before an event. Every dinner should be carb-based, to refuel the muscles on a daily basis. An athlete can only compete at his best if he trains at his best, and this means fueling-up and refueling on a daily basis.

Sometimes parents think they are serving a high carbohydrate dinner when they actually are serving foods that contribute to "fat loading" and not "carbo-loading." For example, lasagna, fettucini alfredo and pepperoni pizza with double cheese offer more fat and protein than carbohydates. The fat fills the stomach, but leaves the muscles poorly fueled.

Better pre-game meal choices would be thick crust pizza with little cheese (and veggie toppings), or spaghetti with tomato sauce and a few meatballs. Carbohydrate-rich desserts include lowfat frozen yogurt (instead of ice cream), fig newtons or pop tarts (instead of butter-laden cookies), and juice pops.

The morning of an event, your child should eat breakfast. Despite popular belief, the food eaten even five minutes before exercise can actually help, and not hurt, athletic performance. Breakfast helps maintain a normal blood sugar; this enhances energy, feeds the brain, and helps the athlete stay focused and better able to concentrate on the event.

Your child should not eat too much—nor too little—of tried foods that settle well. The exact amount to eat is hard to pinpoint; portions will vary according to an athlete's individual ability to tolerate pre-exercise food. Some children will be so nervous the thought of food will make them nauseous. (In which case, they should eat "breakfast"—or a substantial snack—before they go to bed the night before.) Others will perform better with familiar foods. Some popular pre-exercise breakfast choices include:

- cereal with milk and a banana;
- bagel and a yogurt;
- toast, with just a little margarine or light cream cheese and some lowfat milk or juice;
- oatmeal with raisins and lowfat milk.

Fluids: Water, juice, and sports drinks

Your child is unlikely to become dehydrated during normal play and activity. But young athletes who engage in competitive, nonstop physical activity lasting more than 30 to 40 minutes (youth soccer, football, basketball) are at higher risk for becoming overheated and dehydrated than are adults who exercise at the same rate for a similar amount of time. Children have a greater body surface area in respect to their body weight, so they gain heat faster from the environment than do adults. They also produce more body heat at a given running speed, and they sweat less than adults do. (Each sweat gland produces about 40% less sweat than an adult sweat gland.) All of this means: Encourage your active children to drink frequently to help regulate their body temperature!

A child's fluid needs are best met by water and milk, although fruit juice in limited quantities is good and can provide valuable nutrients. Childrens' growing bodies need lowfat milk (for calcium, protein) and some juice (for Vitamin C and other health-enhancing nutrients). They don't need soda pop or other sugar-filled beverages, given the plethora of sugar-laden foods that are readily available for kids to eat.

Provide palatable fluids (milk, juice, ice water) throughout the day, particularly before and after exercise. Your child doesn't have to drink plain water, per se, to get the fluids she needs. Plain water is one source of water; lemonade, watermelon, salads and vegetables, soups, yogurt, milk and other watery foods are other good sources.

Consumption of sports drinks should be limited to during actual sporting events, and not used as a routine beverage. If your child wants sports drinks at other times, such as in her lunch box or for snacks, I say "bad choice." Sports drinks are just sugar water with a little added salt (sodium). They are not a nutritious addition to a child's diet. While they are helpful to maintain energy when taken during exercise that lasts for more than an hour in the heat, most kids are unlikely to be training at that level. Whether or not your child really "needs" a sports drink depends on the need to optimize hydration.

- Kids at play are unlikely to need a sports drink because they generally do not sweat enough to become dehydrated. Teach your child how to tell if she is drinking adequate fluids: voiding a significant volume of pale yellow urine every 2 to 4 hours. (Note: If she takes vitamin supplements, her urine may be bright yellow, but it should still have adequate volume.)

- If your kids are involved in sports that are played for extended times in the heat, and if they are sweating heavily, you do need to optimize their fluid intake. The best way to prevent dehydration and optimize fluid intake is to provide cool fluids that taste good. Research suggests kids drink more of a sports drink than they do of plain water. In this situation, the investment in sports drinks may be worthwhile. [Note: if your child is overweight or obese it is best to avoid sugar drinks—use water.]

- If your children are involved in high intensity sports such as soccer, basketball, and hockey, they may perform better if they consume a sports drink *during* the exercise session. The sports drink provides not only water but also energy—and helps maintain stamina and boost performance.

In general, active kids who sweat heavily should pay careful attention to their fluid intake. They should not rely upon thirst alone to tell how much they need to drink, because the thirst mechanism may poorly reflect actual fluid needs. Research suggests athletes tend to voluntarily replace only half their water losses.

If your child is a heavy sweater, I recommend he determine his sweat rate by weighing himself naked before and after he exercises. Given that one pound of lost sweat equals two cups of fluid, he should plan to replace his sweat losses accordingly. For example, if he drops one pound of sweat during exercise, he should target drinking at least one pound (16 ounces) of fluids during future exercise bouts.

To insure optimal re-hydration, he should routinely consume plenty of fluids throughout the day. At home, keep an inviting supply of water, juice or fruit smoothies in the refrigerator. If he enjoys the taste of the fluid, he'll drink more.

Growing bones need calcium-rich foods

Milk, yogurt and cheese are a major source of calcium for growing bones (as well as of protein, for growth and muscles). Growing children need a serving of (soy) milk, yogurt or cheese at each meal to consume adequate calcium; that's three servings of calcium-rich food per day. One serving is equivalent to:

8 ounces milk
8 ounces soy milk, calcium-fortified
1.5 ounces cheese
1 cup (8 ounces) yogurt, all flavors.

When possible, choose reduced fat dairy foods, such as 1% milk, lowfat yogurt, lowfat chocolate milk or reduced fat cheese. Calcium-fortified orange juice is another calcium source, but it lacks the protein found in regular or soy milk. Calcium-fortified soy milk is a fine alternative to cow's milk.

Protein needs

Adequate protein is very important for normal growth, and in building strong muscles. Growing children may need 0.5 to 1.0 grams of protein per pound (1.0-1.5 gm protein/ kg) of body weight, per day. This comes to 40 to 75 grams of protein for a 10 year old who weighs 75 pounds. This equates to the protein from three servings of milk or yogurt plus some protein-rich food at two meals per day. For example, your child can easily get the right amount of protein by consuming daily:

* three 8-ounce glasses of milk (30 grams of protein) plus
* a sandwich at lunch (15 gms) plus
* some protein-rich food at dinner, such as spaghetti with meat sauce (15 gms).

Note: If your child drinks juice or soda in place of milk at meals, and routinely eats meatless pasta dinners, she may lack protein.

Adequate protein supports growth, but extra protein will not build bigger muscles. The hormones that kick-in at puberty create muscular bulk. Even kids who strength train (light to moderate resistance to reduce stress on the ligaments and joints) won't bulk-up by adding excess protein to the diet.

Examples of protein-rich foods:
* meat or poultry
* fish, including canned tuna
* eggs
* dried beans and legumes, including hummus, chili, refried beans, lentil soup, chick peas, split peas and canned beans
* tofu and foods made with soy, such as soy dogs, soy burgers, soy "chicken" nuggets, nuts and seeds, including almond, peanuts, peanut butter, sunflower seeds, sesame seeds
* milk, yogurt

Despite popular belief, eating lean red meat (such as beef, pork and lamb) three to four times a week (1-2 lunches, 1-2 dinners) can be a positive part of a child's sports diet. Red meats help maintain iron levels in growing children whose blood volume is expanding.

Because the fat in meat is unhealthy and contributes to the development of heart disease, the trick is to choose lean meats, such as a lean roast beef sandwich, extra-lean hamburger in spaghetti sauce, and beef stir-fry, but limit the intake of greasy burgers, sausage and pepperoni. If you have concerns about the possible use of hormones and antibiotics in standard meats, then allay your concerns by buying lean meats at a natural foods store.

Note: target meats that have less than 30% of the calories in fat, compared to the total number of calories in a portion of the food.

Iron and zinc
Red meats and darker fish (salmon, tuna) supply not only protein but also iron and zinc.

- Iron is an important part of red blood cells, and helps transport oxygen from the lungs to the working muscles. Kids who consume too little iron can become anemic and fatigue easily when exercising. If your child does not eat red meats, iron-enriched breakfast cereals are an alternate iron source.
- Zinc is involved in growth and healing. Zinc tends to be found in many of the same foods that contain iron.

Smart kids eat breakfast

Children who skip breakfast generally miss out on important nutrients, to say nothing of fuel to enjoy a high energy day and be able to concentrate at school and sports. Breakfast skippers tend to consume less calcium, iron, dietary fiber, vitamins and the calories needed for energy. If there's "no time" for breakfast at home, breakfast should be eaten at the bus stop or while driving to school.

Some kid-friendly breakfast ideas include:
- toast with peanut butter, banana and hot cocoa (made with milk)
- leftover cheese pizza
- cereal with milk and berries
- granola bar plus a yogurt and orange juice
- oatmeal with raisins and milk

Kids and "junk food"

Most active children can meet their nutrient needs within 1,200 to 1,500 calories of a variety of wholesome foods. This will allow for small portions of "junk food" (fatty or sugary treats). Avoid the timing of these snacks so that you won't reduce the appetite for nutritious meals. This is particularly important if your child eats a poor lunch at school. You don't have control over your child's eating at school, so try to feed defensively when you have the chance.

Don't try to restrict all junky treats (foods with sugar, fat and little nutritional value). Children generally can thrive on a diet with about 30% of the calories from fat. If they eat significantly less fat, they may not consume adequate calories. They can also enjoy about 10% of their calories from sugar (200 calories of sugar per day for a child who requires 2,000 calories). Preferably, the sugar will come along with somewhat healthful foods, such as apple crisp, oatmeal-raisin cookies, lowfat yogurt, and chocolate milk. While parents may be tempted to refer to foods as being "good" or "bad," in reality, one needs to look at the whole diet. For example, eating too many apples (a "good" food) can create a "bad diet" by limiting the intake of a variety of other foods that contribute to a balanced diet.

Fitness for fat kids: Weight and dieting

Some parents may be tempted to force their (chubby) kids to exercise as part of a weight loss plan. Some weight conscious children may embrace a running program as a way to stay thin; dieting is common even among third graders. In a California study, 30-46% of 9 year old girls–and 46-81% of 10 year olds–had disordered eating behavior.

Parents take heed: dieting (and exercising to lose undesired body fat) is not just about "getting healthy"; it is about feeling "not good enough," having a poor self-image, and low self-esteem. As a parent, you need to downplay a child's body size as an important currency of worth, and instead value and accept individual differences. Never comment about the size of large children; your child will conclude she/he must be thin to be valued and loved, and will start dieting. This is particularly important with young girls who are coping with body changes. Their efforts to control weight may lead to a sense of frustration, guilt, despair, and failure. Unfortunately, it can also lead to a pattern of unhealthy eating disorders.

If your child is overweight: What's a parent to do?

As a parent, you can be a good role model for regular exercise and healthful food choices. But when it comes to controlling your children's eating and exercise practices, you are likely to feel more and more out of control with each passing year. Once your overweight child is old enough to march off to CVS to spend his or her allowance on candy, chips and soft drinks, what can you do to regain control without becoming the food police?

The answer is complex, under-researched, and a topic of debate among parents and pediatricians alike. We know that restricting a child's food intake does not work. Rather, restricting kids' food tends to result in sneak-eating, binge-eating, guilt, shame—the same stuff that adults encounter when they "blow their diets." But this time, the parents become the food police—and this creates an undesirable family dynamic.

Food restrictions cause problems

Despite your best intentions to prevent creeping obesity, do not put your overweight child on a diet, deprive him of french fries, nor ban candy. Dietary restrictions don't work – not for adults, and not for kids. Think about this: If diets did work, then the majority of people who have dieted would all be lean. That's far from the case.

Diets for children cause more problems than they solve. They disrupt a child's natural ability to eat when hungry and stop when content. Instead, the child overcompensates and doesn't stop when he's content (binges) or stuffs himself with "last chance eating." You know, "Last chance to have birthday cake so I'd better eat a lot now because when I get home where I'm restricted to celery sticks and rice cakes."

If you are the parent of a chubby child, note that children commonly grow out before they grow up. That is, they often gain body fat before embarking on a growth spurt. Instead of putting your daughter on a diet (which damages self-esteem and imprints the message she isn't good enough the way she is), get her involved in sports and other activities.

You can delicately ask if she is comfortable with her body. If she is discontent with her physique and expresses a desire to learn how to eat better, arrange for a consultation with a registered dietitian who specializes in pediatric weight control. (Use the American Dietetic Association's referral network at www.eatright.org.) A great resource is Ellyn Satter's, *Your Child's Weight: Helping Without Harming and Secrets of Feeding a Healthy Family*.

Is your child really overweight?
If you are feeling anxious about your child's weight, get some professional advice from the pediatrician to determine if the problem is real. You must remember the body a daughter has as a 10 year old will change as she grows and develops. You can also monitor your child's weight on charts available at www.cdc.gov/growth charts.

Some parents are rightly concerned about their child's weight; we're seeing more and more medical problems with childhood diabetes, high cholesterol, and high blood pressure. But for other parents, the concern about their child's weight reflects their own anxiety about having an "imperfect" kid. Yes, you say you want to spare your child the grief of being fat –but be sure to also examine your own issues. If you yourself are very weight-conscious and put a high value on how you look, you may be feeling blemished if your child is fat. Often, the child's weight problem is really the parent's issue. Many parents over-react when a child gains only a few pounds before the growth spurt. Check with your child's doctor.

Be sure to love your overweight child from the inside out—and not judge him from the outside in. Realize that comments such as, "That dress is pretty, honey, but it would look even better if you'd just lose a few pounds....." get interpreted as "I'm not good enough." Self-esteem takes a nose-dive and contributes to anorexic thinking, such as "thinner is better."

Weight management tips

So what can you do to help fat kids slim-down? Instead of maligning them and trying to get them thin by restricting food, help them to become healthier by encouraging physical activity. This could mean watching less TV, training for a family fun run, planning enjoyable family activities (unlike boot camp), and perhaps even creating a "walking school bus" with the neighborhood kids. As a family, you might want to participate in a charitable walking or running event.

As part of a society, make your voice heard about the need for safe sidewalks, health clubs that welcome overweight kids, swimming pools that allow children (and adults, for that matter) to wear T-shirts and shorts instead of embarrassing bathing suits.

Food-wise, provide your kids with wholesome, nourishing foods, as well as semi-regular "junk foods." (Otherwise, they will go out and get them). Encourage them to eat breakfast. Plan structured meals and snacks; take dinnertime seriously. Your job is to determine the what, where and when of eating; the child's job is to determine **how much** and **whether** to eat. (That is, don't force them to finish their peas, nor stop them from having second helpings.) If you interfere with a child's natural ability to regulate food, you can cause a lifetime of struggles. Trust them to eat when hungry, stop when content—and have plenty of energy to enjoy an active lifestyle. If this feels difficult to you, be sure to read Ellyn Satter's, *Your Child's Weight: Helping Without Harming* and *Secrets of Feeding a Healthy Family*. Ellyn is the expert on how to feed kids in today's challenging food environment.

How to gain weight healthfully

Not all kids are fat. In fact, many are skinny and struggle to eat enough calories for both sports and growth. To gain weight, your child needs to consume more calories than he currently eats. He can:
- drink more calories (such as enjoy a taller glass of milk),
- eat an extra snack (such as a bedtime peanut butter and jelly sandwich) or
- eat larger portions at meals (two potatoes instead of one).

But please don't serve him lots of fatty foods like extra french fries and ice cream!

For the easiest way to gain weight, I recommend your child consistently drink more healthful fluids. Juice is a super choice, as is lowfat milk.
- Juice provides carbohydrates to fuel muscles, plus fluid to replace sweat losses. Cranapple (or any cran-flavor) and grape are particularly good choices because they are calorie-dense. I had one client who gained 13 pounds over the summer by trading in water for cranapple juice; he drank a half-gallon bottle per day, in addition to maintaining his typical food intake.
- Lowfat milk (your choice of 2%, 1%, or skim) also provides carbs and fluids—with a bonus of protein for building muscles. Add some chocolate flavoring for more carbs and calories.

The trick in gaining weight is to ***consistently*** consume extra calories in order to achieve weight gain, and this requires dedication. You can find more detailed information about how to gain weight healthfully in my *Sports Nutrition Guidebook.* (www.nancyclarked.com)

Sports dietitian Nancy Clark, MS, RD counsels both casual exercisers and competitive athletes at her successful private practice at Healthworks Fitness Center (617-383-6100) in Chestnut Hill, MA. Her best-selling **Sports Nutrition Guidebook**, *as well as her* **Food Guide for Marathoners: Tips for Everyday Champions**, *offer additional fueling information that can help parents appropriately feed their active children.*

The books are available at **www.nancyclarkrd.com.**

Why Does Your Body Want To Hold onto Fat?

Fat is our biological insurance policy against disaster. It is the fuel your body can use, in case of starvation, sickness, injury to the digestive system, etc. You'll read a bit later about how your biological "set point" programs your body to hold onto fat at any age. Strenuous exercise is one of the few ways than anyone can at least keep the fat level from rising, and may help in reducing. I've spent years looking into this topic, and talking to experts in the field. This chapter will explain my beliefs about the process so that you can set up a strategy, based upon the needs and goals of you and your family. Then, you can take control over a major part of this process.

Any exercise that you like or your child enjoys can burn fat. The best fat burners, for time-efficiency are walking and running. My run-walk method is an extremely effective and convenient exercise mode for using your fat storage to provide energy for exercise. This method has helped thousands learn to enjoy endurance exercise— which acts like a fat-burning furnace. When the body is conditioned for fat burning, it prefers this as fuel, because of the small amount of waste product produced.

But it's not enough to burn the fat. For long term health and body management, you need to keep it off. Successful fat burners do four things:

1. Understand the process by reading this chapter and other sources.
3. Truly believe that they can maintain or lower the body fat percentage.
4. Set up a behavioral plan that fits into the lifestyle and increase exercise.
5. Control the income side of the equation.

How does fat accumulate?

When you eat some fat during a snack or a meal, you might as well put it into a syringe and inject it into your stomach or thigh. A gram of fat eaten is a gram of fat deposited in the fat storage areas on your body. In addition, when you eat more calories than you burn during a day, from protein (fish, chicken, beef, tofu) and carbohydrate (breads, fruits, vegetables, sugar), the excess is converted into fat and stored.

Fat for survival

More than a million years of evolution have programmed the human body to hold on to the fat you have stored due to a powerful principle: the survival of the species. Before humans understood how to reduce and fight disease, they were susceptible to sweeping infections. Even mild infections and flu wiped out a significant percentage of the population, regularly, in primitive times. Those who had adequate fat stores survived periods of starvation and sickness, produced children, and passed on the fat accumulation adaptation.

The powerful set point holds onto our fat

The set point is a biologically engineered survival mechanism. While it does seem possible to adjust it, you are going into battle against survival mechanisms that have been in place for over a million years. The tools in this chapter can help you understand the process and take action to adjust your set point.

Fat level is set in early 20s

Many experts agree that by about the age of 25, we have accumulated a level of fat that the body intuitively marks as it's lowest level. This "set point" is programmed to increase a little each year. Let's say that John had 10% body fat at age 25, and his set point increased by half a percent per year. The amount of increase is so small when we are young, that we usually don't realize that it is increasing each year—until a decade later, when it's time to go to a class reunion.

We humans are supposed to carry around fat. But your set point does too good a job, continuing to add to the percentage, each year, every year. And the amount of increase becomes greater as we get older. Unfortunately, the set point has a good memory. When you've had a tough year due to stress or illness and didn't add the usual increase, the set point over-compensates by increasing appetite during the following year or two. Go ahead, shout "Unfair!" as loud as you wish. Your set point doesn't argue, it just makes another deposit. But there's hope through exercise.

Men and women deposit fat differently

While men tend to deposit fat on the surface of the skin, women (particularly in their 20's and 30's) fill up internal storage areas first. Most girls and women will acknowledge that their weight is rising slightly, year by year, but aren't concerned because there is no noticeable fat increase on the outside. The "pinch test" is how many people monitor their fat increase—and is not adequate.

When the internal storage areas fill up, the extra fat accumulates on the stomach, thighs and other areas. A common woman's complaint in the 30's or early 40's is the following: "My body has betrayed me." In fact, fat has often been deposited at a fairly consistent rate but hidden from view for many years.

Men usually find it easier to burn fat than women

When men start endurance exercise, such as running, many lose fat and weight for several months. Probably related to biological issues, and primitive protections for mothers, women have a harder time losing it. The reality is that you are ahead of the others in our society....even if you are maintaining the same weight. Because of the set point, one would expect an average 45 year old person in the U.S. to gain about 4 pounds a year. So maintaining weight and holding the set point steady is a huge fat management victory.

Diets don't work because of the "starvation reflex"

We are certainly capable lowering food intake for days, weeks and months to lower fat levels and weight. This is a form of starvation and the set point has a long-term memory. Many folks diet and lose 10 pounds during the 2 months before the class reunion. Then, when the diet ends, the starvation rebound occurs: a slight increase in appetite and hunger occurs, over weeks and months, until the fat percentage accumulated on your body is higher that it was before the diet. It's a fact that almost all of those who lose fat on a diet put more pounds back on the body within months of going off the diet.

The starvation reflex: Waiting too long to eat triggers it

When you wait more than three hours without eating something, your set point organism senses that you may be going into a period of starvation. The longer you wait to eat, the more you will feel these three effects of the starvation reflex:

1. **A reduction in your metabolism rate.** Imagine an internal voice saying something like this, "If this person is going to start depriving me of food I had better dial down the metabolism rate to conserve resources." A slower metabolism makes you feel more lethargic, drowsy, and unmotivated to exercise or move around. In fact, most respond by staying in their chair or the couch, minimizing motion and calorie burning.

2. **An increase in the fat-depositing enzymes.** The longer you wait to eat something, the more enzymes are produced. The next time you eat, a greater percentage of the meal will be deposited on your body.

3. **Your appetite increases.** The longer you wait to eat, the more likely it is that, for the next few meals, you will have a greater-than-usual appetite: After a normal meal, you're still hungry.

Suddenly depriving yourself of decadent foods

I used to like a particular type of ice cream so much that I ate a quart or more of it, several nights a week. It was the reward I gave myself for reaching my exercise goals for that day. Then, on a fateful New Year's day, my wife Barb and I decided to eliminate the chocolate chip mint ice cream from our diet—after more than 10 years of enjoyment. We were successful for two years. A leftover box after a birthday party got us re-started on the habit, and we even increased our intake over what it had been before—due to having deprived ourselves.

You can "starve" yourself of a food that you dearly love for an extended period of time. But at some time in the future, when the food is around and no one else is.....you will tend to over-consume that food. My correction for this problem was the following:

1. I made a contract with myself: I could have a little of it whenever I wanted—while promising to be "reasonable."
2. I set a goal of enjoying one bowl a week, five years in the future.
3. Four years ahead, the goal was enjoying a bowl every five days.
4. Three years ahead, a bowl every four days.
5. Learning to enjoy healthy sweet things, like fruit salads, energy bars, etc.

It worked! I hardly ever eat any ice cream...but sometimes enjoy a bowl if I want. This is purely for medicinal reasons, you understand.

The low-carbohydrate scam

There is no doubt that low-carb diets can help you lose weight....water weight. Such a loss is superficial and easily gained back. Here's how it works. To perform physical exertion, you need a quick energy source (for the first 15 minutes) called glycogen, which comes from eating carbohydrates, and must be replenished every day. The storage areas for glycogen are limited and glycogen is also the primary source for vital organs like the brain. About four times the amount of water is stored near the glycogen storage areas, because it is needed when glycogen is processed into energy.

By starving themselves of carbohydrates, low-carb dieters experience a severe reduction in glycogen stores. But if the glycogen isn't there, water storage is also reduced. The elimination of these two substances can produce a significant weight loss within days—continuing for a few weeks.

Fat is not being burned off. In fact, fat consumption is encouraged in many of the low-carb diets. As low-carb dieters eat more fat, they often increase the fat on the body, while the water/glycogen loss will show a weight loss, due to the superficial loss of water. When water and glycogen are replaced later, the weight goes back on. Soon, the overall body weight is greater than before because of the extra fat gained during the low-carb diet.

Because the glycogen energy source is low or depleted, low carbers will have little energy for exercise. This is why you will hear folks on this diet complain about how tired they are, with no desire to exercise. When they try to run, they can't finish a workout, and usually experience lack of mental focus (low glycogen means less fuel for the brain).

Even if you "tough it out" or cheat on the diet a little, your capacity to do even moderately strenuous exertions will be greatly reduced. With your energy stores near empty, exercising becomes a real struggle, and no fun.

Low-carb diet literature doesn't tell you this....
- You don't burn fat—many gain fat.
- The weight loss is usually water loss, with glycogen loss.
- Almost everyone on this diet resumes regular eating within a few weeks or months.
- Almost all low-carb dieters gain back more weight than they lost.
- You lose the energy and motivation to exercise.

- You lose exercise capacity that can help to keep the weight off when you resume eating normally.
- Your metabolism rate goes down—making it harder to keep the weight off.

This is a type of starvation diet. I've heard from countless low-carb victims who admit that while they were on the diet, their psychological deprivation of carbs produced a significant rebound effect when they began eating them again. The cravings for bread, pastries, french fries, soft drinks, and other pound-adding foods, increased for months. The weight goes back on, and on, and on.

Like so many diets, the low-carb diet reduces the metabolism rate. This reduces the number of calories you burn per day, just living. When you return to eating a regular diet you will not have a "metabolism furnace" to burn up the increased calories.

Lowering the set point

Your body has a wonderful ability to adapt to the regular activities that you do. It also tries to avoid stress. In the next chapter we will talk about how to condition your muscles to be fat burning furnaces. Once you get them into shape to do this, you can move into a fat burning lifestyle. Lowering the set point is more complex, but possible—when you are regularly putting certain types of stress on your system.

Endurance walking and running: a positive stress which can stimulate adaptations in two areas

Running/walking regularly, long enough to produce these stresses, will trigger a search for ways of reducing the stress.
- body temperature increase
- pounding or bouncing

The temperature increase from running/walking helps you to reduce the set point

Everyone knows that when you run, you get warm or hot. The work required to lift your body off the ground raises your core body temperature—even when you have liberal walk breaks. While this is usually not a health risk, if you sustain this artificial fever, at least every other day for more than about 45 minutes, you're putting a heat stress on the system. Since body fat acts like a blanket in maintaining body temperature, the body's intuitive, long term solution, is to reduce the size of this fat blanket, which then reduces the heat buildup.

The more regular you are with run-walks that build up to more than 45 minutes, the more likely it is that your set point will be reduced to avoid this repeated stress. It also helps even more to have one run-walk every week that goes beyond 90 minutes.

Bouncing and pounding

The more weight you carry, the more you will feel the pounding effect of running. If you run as often as every other day, your body senses this regular stress and searches for ways of reducing it. It will tend to adapt by reducing the extra fat baggage, reducing the bounce stress.

Cross training for fat burning

To maintain a regular dose of set-point lowering stress, while minimizing orthopedic stress, cross training can help. The best activities are those that raise core body temperature, use a lot of muscle cells, and can be continued comfortably for more than 45 minutes. Swimming is not a good fat-burning exercise. The water absorbs temperature buildup, and therefore core body temperature doesn't rise significantly.

Good fat burning cross-training exercises
- Nordic track
- Walking
- Elliptical
- Rowing
- Exercise cycle

How to Burn More Fat—Today

"By running and walking for at least 90 minutes during one session each week, the leg muscles become fat burners. Over time, this means that you will burn more fat when you are sitting around all day at your desk and even burn it when you are sleeping at night."

Slow, aerobic running and walking are two of the very best ways to burn fat. But most runners, during their first year, usually hold their own, showing no weight loss. This is actually a victory over the set point. By not gaining any fat, runners are beating the set point increase of about 3-4 pounds a year. But runners are actually burning fat when they maintain weight. How can this be? Read on.

As you run, you increase the storage of glycogen and water, all over the body, to process energy and cool you down. Your blood volume also increases. All of these internal changes help you exercise better, but will increase your body weight (not a fat gain). If your weight is the same, a year after starting endurance exercise, you have burned off several pounds of fat. Don't let the scales drive you crazy.

Long term fat burn-off requires discipline and focus. If you will take responsibility for managing your eating and doing the running and walking needed, you will succeed. One secret to fat burning success is being more active all day long. Once you learn to walk instead of sit, you will be amazed at how many steps you can take per day

Aerobic running burns fat

By taking liberal walk breaks, and running totally within your physical capacity (no huffing and puffing), your muscles are being supplied with enough oxygen to do the work: You are aerobic. If you run too hard you overwhelm the capacity of the muscles, and the blood system cannot deliver enough oxygen to the muscles: you are anaerobic (you're not getting enough oxygen to burn fat as fuel).

Slow running burns fat, and fast running burns sugar (glycogen).

Oxygen is needed to burn fat. Therefore running at an easy pace will keep you in the aerobic, or "fat burning" zone. When you run too fast, for that day, and your muscles can't get enough oxygen, you will huff and puff. This is the sign that you are building up an oxygen debt. Without oxygen, the muscles turn to stored glycogen as fuel, which produces a high amount of waste product.

Fat burning training program

- One slow, long run-walk a week of 60 min + (90 min + is better)
- Two other slow run-walks of 45 min +
- 2-3 cross training sessions of 45 min +
- Taking an additional 6-10,000 (or more) steps a day in your daily activities

Sugar-burning during the first 15 min of exercise

Glycogen is the quick access fuel your body uses during the first quarter hour of exercise. Those who don't exercise longer than 15 minutes will not get into fat burning, and won't train their muscles to burn this fuel. But if you have been depriving yourself of carbohydrates, as when on a low-carb diet, you won't have enough fuel to burn and will struggle to find energy and motivation for the first 15 minutes.

When glycogen is used for fuel, it produces a significant waste product—mostly lactic acid. If you move slowly, mostly walking, there is no significant buildup. Even when the pace feels slow, if you are huffing and puffing within the first 10 minutes, you have been going too fast (for you, on that day). When in doubt, extend your walking at the beginning and go slower.

From 15 minutes to 45 minutes you will transition into fat burning

If you are exercising within your capabilities, after 15 minutes your body starts to break down body fat, and use it as fuel. Fat is actually a more efficient fuel, producing less waste product. This transition continues for the next 30 minutes or so. By the time you've been exercising within your capabilities for 45-50 minutes, you will be burning mostly fat—if the muscles are trained to do this. With lots of walking, and a slow pace, almost anyone can work up to three sessions of 45 minutes each.

Three sessions a week, in the fat burn zone

Even the most untrained muscles that have only burned glycogen for 50 years can be trained to burn fat under two conditions:

- Exercise easily, and get into the fat-burning zone (45+ minutes each session)
- Do this regularly: 3 times a week. (best to have no more than two days between sessions)

One session a week beyond 90 minutes

The longer session should gradually increase up to an hour and half—keeping you in the fat burn zone long enough to encourage your muscles to adapt to fat burning. For best results, this should be done every week. If you don't have time for a 90 minute session, shoot for at least 60 minutes.

Walk breaks allow you to go farther without getting tired

This pushes you into the fat burn zone while allowing for a quick recovery of the muscles. For fat-burning purposes, it is best to walk earlier, and walk more often. The number of calories you burn is based upon the number of miles covered. Walk breaks allow you to cover more distance each day, without tiring yourself. By lowering the exertion level, you will stay in the fat burning zone longer— usually for the whole session. When in doubt, it's best to walk more and slow down.

Be realistic with yourself. Are you willing to make the lifestyle changes you'll need to burn significant fat? If you're not sure, use some of the suggestions in this chapter and look at the big picture: Even if you don't lose a pound, running regularly will give you a series of health benefits. Studies at the Cooper Clinic, founded by

Dr. Kenneth Cooper in Dallas, Texas and other organizations, have shown that even obese people lower their risk factors for heart disease when they exercise regularly—and are often much healthier than thin people who don't exercise.

BMI Can Monitor Obesity Risk

"Children at the highest levels of BMI are generally at the greatest risk of adverse health outcomes."
Preventing Childhood Obesity, by the Institute of Medicine of the National Academies.

A high percentage of parents don't know that their kids are overweight or obese. It's part of the human condition to want to avoid bad news. Those who sense that they are overweight often go into a "cut off the head of the messenger" strategy. Since the results of inaction are deadly, and the benefits for taking action are significant and continuing, it pays to take action—-it's the right thing to do.

The system in this book involves giving you a simple way to measure the key markers, so that you can discretely identify someone who is at risk, and track improvement. Those who follow the simple and gentle training methods and food management suggestions will almost always see progress.

What is the BMI? It is a simple computation of your "body mass index" using current weight and height. This has become the basic test to determine whether someone is overweight or obese. You can use the figure gained in this computation to track progress. To see whether a child is at risk, ask your doctor. Another reference is the following website page: www.cdc.gov/growth charts.

The monthly "Progress Check" (PC)
Mark one day each month as your PC day. Try to be aware of possible schedule interruptions on the proposed day, so that nothing will interfere with this. Make it fun by making it easy for each person to do, with a healthy snack afterward. It is important

to use the same scale on each progress check. Be sure to explain the meaning of BMI, how you compute it, and recognize those who have made progress.

Adult BMI formula:

Inches/pounds: (weight in pounds) divided by (height in inches, squared) times 703
Example: 100 pound person that is 5 feet tall—100 divided by 3600 x 703 = 19.52 BMI
Example: 200 pound person that is 5 feet tall—200 divided by 3600 x 703 = 39.05

Meters/kilograms: (weight in kilograms) divided by (height in meters, squared)
Example: 100 kilogram person that is 2 meters tall—100 divided by 4 = 25
Example: 160 kilogram person that is 2 meters tall—160 divided by 4 = 40

1. This is a simple and indirect way of measuring body fat—the higher the number, the more body fat.

2. You need an accurate scale—and you need to use the same scale.

3. The best time to weigh is right after rising in the morning. At school, the first period or right before lunch is another good time. Even if you measure at different times, there are usually only incidental changes.

4. Set aside a specific day each month to do BMI and write it on the calendar.

5. Weight is the key element. Height will not change in adults and will change very slowly with children.

Adults with a BMI of 25 to 29.9 are considered "overweight". When the BMI exceeds 30, the classification changes to obese.

Children (2-18 years old) who are above the 94.9th percentile in BMI charts for age/gender are designated as obese. Talk to your children's doctor to determine your child's BMI percentage. You can also check the CDC information: www.cdc.gov/growth charts

Arkansas takes the lead! The Arkansas State Legislature passed a law in 2003, requiring schools to provide parents with each child's BMI with an explanation of what it means, and information on the health effects of obesity.

Fat Burning Training: for the Rest of Your Life

"The bottom line in fat burning: # of calories burned per week."

How much walking and how much running?

By inserting more walk breaks into all runs, you can cover more miles without increasing fatigue.

Follow the guidelines in the Galloway Run-Walk-Run Method segment. When in doubt, walk more. It is also better to choose a ratio that seems too easy for you—so you'll recover fast.

10,000 walking steps a day on non exercise days/6000 on exercise days

Adding walking steps to your day may burn more fat off your body than running. While running sets up the fat-burning process, it may trigger an appetite increase. Walking doesn't increase appetite significantly. A pedometer, or step counter will provide an incentive to walk more, and reinforcement for adding extra steps to your day. No other device that I know will give you a sense of control over your actual calorie burn-off. Once you get into the goal of taking more than 10,000 steps a day in your everyday activities, you'll find yourself getting out of your chair more often, parking farther away from the supermarket, walking around the kid's playground, etc.

Step counters are usually about one inch square, and clip onto your belt, pocket or waistband. The simple models just count steps and this is all you need. Other models compute miles and calories. I recommend getting one from a quality manufacturer. When tested, some of the lower quality models registered 3-4 times as many steps as the quality products did—walking exactly the same course. For recommendations on step counters, see my website: www.JeffGalloway.com.

Your goal is to accumulate at least 10,000 walking steps at home, at work, going shopping, waiting for kids, parents etc., on your non-running days (6000 on your running days). This is very doable. You will find many pockets of time during the day when you are just sitting or standing. As you increase the step count, you become a more active person and feel more energized.

About dinnertime, do a "step check." If you haven't acquired your 10,000 (or 6000), walk around the block a few extra times before or after the meal. You don't have to stop with these figures. As you get into it, you'll find many more opportunities to walk….and burn.

Up to 59 pounds of fat….gone in one year

The fat wars are won by many small burning skirmishes: a little here, and a little there. Most of us have many opportunities. I've heard from many folks who took advantage of many of the following loopholes, every day, and burned off dozens of pounds in a year.

Pounds burned per year/Activity

1-2 pounds	taking the stairs instead of the elevator
10-30 pounds	getting out of your chair at work to walk down the hall
1-2 pounds	getting off the couch to move around the house (but not to get potato chips)

1-2 pounds	parking farther away from the supermarket, mall, etc
1-3 pounds	parking farther away from your work
2-4 pounds	walking around the kid's playground, practice field, doctor's office
2-4 pounds	walking up and down the concourse as you wait for your next flight
3-9 pounds	walking the dog each day
2-4 pounds	walking a couple of times around the block after supper
2-4 pounds	walking a couple of times around the block during lunch hour at work
2-4 pounds	walking an extra loop around the mall, supermarket, etc., to look for bargains (this last one could be expensive when at the mall)
Total: 27-59 pounds a year	

15 more pounds burned each year from adding a few extra miles every week

By using small pockets of time, you can add to your fat-burning without feeling extra fatigue:

- Slow down and add one more mile on each run
- Walk a mile at lunchtime
- Walk or jog a mile before dinner, or afterward

Controlling the Income Side of the Fat Equation

As you get older, your metabolism tends to slow down. Exercise (especially running and walking) will help you "rev-it-up". But gaining control over your calorie intake is crucial for body fat reduction. Runners often complain that even though they have increased mileage, and faithfully done their cross training workouts, they are not losing weight. In every case, when I have questioned them, each did not have a handle on the number of calories they were eating. In every case, when they went through the drill of quantifying, each was eating more than they thought. Below you will find ways to cut 10 or more pounds by diet changes—without starving yourself.

Websites tell you calorie balance and nutrient balance

The best tool I've found for managing your food intake is a good website or software program. There are a number of these that will help to balance your calories (calories burned vs. calories eaten). Most of these will have you log in your exercise for the day, and what you eat. At the end of the day, you can retrieve an accounting of calories, and of nutrients. If you are low on certain vitamins or minerals, protein, etc, after dinner, you can eat food or a vitamin pill.

- Use a website that accounts for age. Your intake will be compared with what is needed for you.
- Some programs will tell vegetarians whether they have received enough complete protein, since this nutrient is harder to put together from vegetable sources.
- If you haven't received enough of some nutrient, you can do something about during the next day to make up the deficit.
- If you ate too many calories, walk after dinner or boost tomorrow's workouts, or reduce the calories, or all of the above.

I don't recommend letting any website control your life. At first, it helps to use it every day for 1-2 weeks. During this time, you'll see patterns, and note where you tend to need supplementation or should cut back. After this initial period, do a spot check, every two weeks or so, for 2-3 days. Some folks need more spot checks than others. If you are more motivated to eat the right foods and quantities by logging in every day, go for it.

For a list of the websites, see my website: www.jeffgalloway.com. Try several out before you decide.

Learning Portion Control—the greatest benefit
Whether you use a website or not, a very productive drill is that of

logging what you eat every day, for a week. Bring a little note pad, and a small scale if you need it. As people record, and then analyze the calories in each portion, they are usually surprised at the number of calories (and fat grams) they are eating. Many foods have fat and simple sugars so well disguised that you don't realize how quickly the calories add up.

After doing this drill for several days you have a tool that can help you adjust the size of your portions. This is a major step in taking control over the income side of the fat equation. Many runners have told me that they resented the first week of logging in, but it became fairly routine after that. Once you get used to doing this, you become aware of what you will be putting in your mouth, and can make better food choices. Now, you're gaining control over your eating behaviors.

Eating every two hours

As mentioned in the previous chapter, if you have not eaten for about three hours, your body senses that it is going into a starvation mode, slows down the metabolism rate while increasing the production of fat-depositing enzymes. This means that you will not be burning as many calories as is normal, that you won't tend to be as mentally and physically alert, and that more of your next meal will be stored away as fat.

You can often burn more fat by eating more often. If the starvation reflex starts working after three hours, then you can beat it by eating every two hours. A person who now eats 2-3 times a day, can burn 8-10 more pounds a year when they shift to eating 8-10 times a day. This assumes that the same calories are eaten using each eating pattern.

Big meals slow you down

Big meals are a big production for the digestive system. Blood is diverted to the long and winding intestine and the stomach. Because of the workload, the body tends to shut down blood flow to other areas, leaving you feeling more lethargic and sedentary. This means that there will be less blood available to the exercising muscles.

Small meals speed you up

Smaller amounts of food can usually be processed quickly without putting a burden on the digestive system. Each time you eat a small meal or snack, your metabolism speeds up. By revving up the metabolism, several times a day, you will burn more calories.

You also give a setback to your set point

When you wait more than three hours between meals, the set point engages the starvation reflex. But if you eat every 2-3 hours, the set point is not engaged—due to the regular supply of food. Therefore, the fat depositing enzymes don't have to be stimulated.

No more tiredness?

Motivation increases when we eat more often. The most common reason I've found for low motivation in the afternoon is not eating regularly enough during the day—especially during the afternoon. If you have not eaten for 4 hours or more, and you're scheduled for exercise that afternoon, you will not feel very motivated—because of low blood sugar and low metabolism. Even when you've had a bad eating day, and feel down in the dumps, you can gear up for a run-walk by having a snack 30-60 minutes before exercise. A fibrous energy bar with water, a cup of coffee (tea, diet drink) can reverse the negative mindset. But you don't have to get yourself into this situation if you eat solid snacks every 2-3 hours.

Satisfaction from a small meal will reduce overeating

The number of calories you eat each day can be reduced by choosing foods (and nutrient combinations) that leave you satisfied longer. Sugar is the worst offender in calorie control and satisfaction. When you drink a beverage with sugar in it, the sugar will be processed very quickly, and you will often be hungry within 30 minutes—even after consuming a high quantity of calories. This will usually lead to two undesirable outcomes:

1. Eating more food to satisfy hunger (calories not needed are processed into fat)
2. Staying hungry and triggering the starvation reflex

Your mission is to find the right combination of foods in your small meals that will leave you satisfied for 2-3 hours. Then, eat another snack that will do the same. You can find a growing number of food combinations that have fewer calories, but keep you from getting hungry until your next snack.

Satisfaction is the key!

Nutrients that leave you satisfied longer:

Fat + Protein + Complex Carbs = SATISFACTION

Eating a snack that has a variety of the three satisfaction ingredients above, will lengthen the time that you'll feel satisfied—even after small meals. These three items take longer to digest, reduce the temptation to eat more calories and, "rev up" the metabolism rate.

Fiber

A greater amount of fiber in foods will slow down digestion. Soluble fiber, such as oat bran, seems to bestow a longer feeling of satisfaction than insoluble fiber such as wheat bran. But any type of fiber will help in this regard.

Fat

Even a little fat, added to a snack, can leave you more satisfied because it slows down digestion. Caution: a little goes a long way. When the fat content of a meal goes beyond 30%, you start to feel more lethargic due to the fact that fat is harder to digest. While up to about 18% of the calories in fat will help you hold hunger at bay, a lot of fat can compromise a fat-burning program. Fat is automatically deposited on your body. None of the dietary fat is used for energy. When you eat a fatty meal, you might as well inject it onto your hips or stomach. The fat you burn as fuel must be broken down from the stored fat on your body. Conclusion: It helps to eat a little fat with a snack, but a lot of it will mean more fat on your body.

There are two kinds of fat that have been found to cause narrowing of the arteries around the heart and leading to your brain: saturated fat and Trans fat. Mono and unsaturated fats, from vegetable sources, are often healthy—olive oil, nuts, avocado, and safflower oil. Some fish oils have Omega 3 fatty acids which have been shown to have a protective effect on the heart. Many fish, however, have oil that is not protective.

Look carefully at the labels. Many foods have vegetable oils that have been processed into Trans fat. A wide range of baked goods and other foods have this negative component. If you have questions, call the 800 number on food packages that don't break down the fat composition—or avoid the food.

Protein—lean protein is best

This nutrient is needed, every day, for the rebuilding of muscle that is broken down during exercise, as well as normal wear and tear. Endurance exercisers don't need to eat significantly more protein than sedentary people. But if they don't get their usual amount of protein, they feel more aches and pains, and a sense of overall weakness, sooner than sedentary people.

Having protein with each meal will leave you feeling satisfied for a longer period of time. But eating more protein calories than you need will produce more body fat.

Recently, protein has been added to sports drinks with great success. When a drink with 80% carbohydrate and 20% protein (such as Accelerade) is consumed within 30 minutes before the start of exercise, glycogen is activated better, and energy is supplied sooner and better. By consuming a drink that has the same ratio (like Endurox R4) within 30 minutes after finishing a run, you'll reload the muscles better and more quickly.

Water

During the parts of the day when you are not exercising, it is best to drink about eight oz of water, about every two hours. The "eight glasses a day" of fluid (recommendation) is a good quota to shoot for. While this is probably more than most people need, I don't see any problems with slight over consumption. You will only get half of the fluid in caffeinated beverages. Alcohol causes dehydration. It's best to minimize alcohol consumption and to add a glass of water to your quota, for each beer or glass of wine consumed.

Complex carbohydrates give you a "discount" and a "grace period"

Foods such as celery, beans, cabbage, spinach, turnip greens, grape nuts, whole grain cereal, etc., can burn up to 25% of the calories in digestion. As opposed to fat (which is directly deposited on your body after eating it), it is only the excess carbs that are processed into fat. After dinner, for example, you have the opportunity to burn off any excess that you acquired during the day by walking around the neighborhood or getting on the treadmill—before it goes into storage.

Recommended percentages of the three nutrients:

There are differing opinions on this issue. Here are the ranges given by a number of top nutritionists that I have read and asked. These are listed in terms of the percentage per day of each of the calories consumed in each nutrient, compared to the total number of calories consumed per day.

Protein:
between 18% and 28%
Fat:
between 15% and 25%
Carbohydrate:
whatever is left—hopefully in complex carbohydrates.

Simple carbs help us put weight back on the body

Fact: We're going to eat some simple carbohydrates. These are the "feel good" foods: candy, baked sweets, starches like mashed potatoes and rice, sugar drinks (including fruit juice and sports drinks) and most desserts. When you are on a fat burning mission you need to minimize the amount of these foods.

The sugar in these products is digested so quickly that you get little or no lasting satisfaction from them. They often leave you with a craving for more of them, which, if denied, will produce a starvation reflex. Because they are processed quickly, you become hungry quickly and will usually eat, accumulating extra calories that usually end up as fat at the end of the day.

As mentioned in the last chapter, it is never a good idea to totally eliminate them by saying something like "I'll never eat another." This sets up a starvation reflex time bomb ticking. Keep taking a bite or two of the foods you dearly love, while cultivating the taste of foods with more fiber and little or no refined sugar or starch.

Good Blood Sugar = Motivation

"Kids who manage blood sugar levels have more energy and better mental focus."

The blood sugar level (BSL) determines how good you feel. When it is stable, you feel energized and motivated. If you eat too much sugar, your BSL can rise too high. You'll feel really good for a while, but the excess sugar triggers a release of insulin, that usually pushes it too low. In this state, you don't have energy, mental focus is foggy, you feel hungry & lazy, and motivation drops rapidly.

When blood sugar level is maintained throughout the day, you will be more motivated to exercise, and feel like adding other movement to your life. Overall, you'll have a more positive mental attitude, and be able to deal with stress and solve problems. Just as eating throughout the day keeps metabolism up, the steady infusion of balanced nutrients, all day long, will maintain stable blood sugar.

You don't want to get on the "bad side" of your BSL. Low levels are a stress on the system and literally mess with your mind. Your brain is fueled by blood sugar and when the supply goes down, your mental stress goes up. If you have not eaten for several hours before a run-walk, you'll receive an increase in the number of negative messages telling you don't have the energy to exercise, that it will hurt, and many others.

The simple act of eating a snack (within 30 minutes of an exercise session) that has carbohydrates and about 20% protein will reduce the negative, make you feel good, and help to push you out the door. Keeping a snack as a BSL booster can often be the difference whether you exercise that day, or not.

The BSL roller coaster

Eating a snack with too many calories of simple carbohydrate can be counter productive for BSL maintenance. As mentioned above, when the sugar level gets too high, your body produces insulin, sending BSL lower than before. The tendency is to eat again, which produces excess calories that are converted into fat. But if you don't eat, you'll stay hungry and miserable—in no mood to exercise or move around and burn calories. People with low blood sugar are no fun to live with.

Eating every 2-3 hours is best

Once you find which snacks work best to maintain your BSL, most people maintain a stable blood sugar level better by eating small meals regularly, every 2-3 hours. As noted in the previous chapter, it's best to combine complex carbs with protein and a small amount of fat.

Do I have to eat before exercise? Only if your blood sugar is low. Most who exercise before breakfast in the morning, don't need to eat anything before the start—unless they have a special condition. As mentioned above, if your blood sugar level is low in the afternoon, and you have exercise scheduled, a snack can help when taken about 30 minutes before. If you feel that a morning snack will help, the only issue is to avoid consuming so much that you get an upset stomach.

For best results in raising blood sugar when it is too low (within 30 minutes before) a snack should have about 80% of the calories in simple carbohydrate and 20% in protein. This promotes the production of insulin, which is helpful (30 min or less) before exercise in getting the glycogen in your muscles ready for action. The product Accelerade has worked best among the thousands of exercisers I hear from every year. It has the 80/20 ratio of carbs to protein. If you eat an energy bar with the 80/20 ratio, be sure to drink 6-8 oz of water.

Eating during exercise

Most exercisers don't need to eat or drink during a workout until the length of the session exceeds 90 minutes. At this point, there are several options. If you are prone to low blood sugar, you may want to start taking your snacks within the first 20 minutes. Most exercisers wait until about 40 minutes before starting.

GU or Gel products—these come in small packets, and are the consistency of honey or thick syrup. The most successful way to take them is to put 1-2 packets in a small plastic bottle with a pop-top. About every 10-15 minutes, take 2-3 small squirts with a sip or two of water. When using the packet, a successful strategy is to take one-third to one-fourth of a packet, every 10-20 minutes.

Energy Bars—Cut into 8-10 pieces and take a piece, with a couple of sips of water, every 10-20 minutes

Candy—particularly gummi bears or hard candies. The usual consumption is 1-2 about every 10 minutes

Sports Drinks—Since there is significant percentage of exercisers who experience nausea when they drink this type of product during exercise, I don't recommend it during a workout. If you have found this to work for you, use it exactly as you have used it before. Even so, these products will add a lot of sugar to your calorie count.

It is important to re-load after exercise—within 30 minutes

Whenever you have finished a hard or long workout (for you), a reloading snack will help you recover faster. Again, the 80/20 ratio of carbs to protein has been most successful in reloading the muscles. This is one situation in which simple carbs are better. The product that has worked best among the thousands I work with each year is Endurox R4.

SUCCESS STORIES

Tina's Story

Tina is one of the bigger girls in her fifth grade class (5' 2" and 160 lbs). Some girls in her class call her fat. As a defense for the hurtful words, Tina counterattacked by saying things about other kids. When Tina reads magazines, all the models are thin, beautiful and sexy. They all have really nice cars and don't have to work when they are fifteen. She's confused. The rich young actresses wear makeup, smoke cigarettes, etc., while her mama, a good strong woman, tells her, "That stuff ain't good for you." But Tina can't help thinking that if she tries it she'll be beautiful too.

Tina joins Girls on the Run. Two thirds of the way through the 12-week program, the girls practice a 3.1 mile run or walk. They have an hour to complete three miles. Tina did not believe she could do it. So like most potential queens, who are frightened, she decided not to try. When her coach yelled "GO," Tina began strolling very slowly around the track. While the majority of girls in the group are running by her, I could see the queen in Tina look on with envy. "My body can never do this," she told herself. At the half hour mark, Tina's coach walked a lap with her, noting that she had covered 1.25 miles and was not going to finish at that pace. But the coach offered hope: with a slight increase in pace, she could.

Tina still had attitude, but responded to the challenge, picking up the pace. With 15 minutes to go, she passes 2 miles. All the other girls have finished, including the fastest, Jordan—a skinny third grader. Jordan was the first to notice something important. She ran to the side of the track where Tina was walking and joyfully said, "Tina, you've gone further than you ever have. Come on, you can do it."

A sparkle came into Tina's eyes. The queen emerged. The realization that "she really could do this" transformed her stroll into a jog, her attitude into an expression of energy and her body into an endurance machine. With every ounce of her being, Tina started jogging first. Huffing and puffing every step of the way, a smile came over her face as she moved that big, strong, bold body around the pavement.

Before the last lap was complete all 16 girls had joined her. She had done it. The body that never would, decided to try. A smile as big as California stretched across that beautiful brown face—sweat breaking out on her brow.

On that day, Tina took her self image back. She took it back from the magazines, from the movies, from MTV, and even from the teacher that told her she was lazy. Tina discovered that she could take control over her body and mind, and create a positive attitude: Big. Strong. Beautiful. Bold.

From Molly Barker, Girls On The Run

On Track For Literacy—Teamworks

Dr. Terri Davis loved running as a kid. It saddened her to see the lower income kids in her hometown of Shreveport, La., just sitting or lying around during the summer—so she invited them to a track meet. How many kids do you think would show up to run in the sultry conditions, when they didn't have to? There were hundreds. These "all comer" meets allowed anyone to run, in any event. So many showed up that she drafted older kids to help organize, and instructed the younger kids in running, jumping, and throwing. The kids loved it and couldn't wait for "track night," so she expanded the program to include two training session a week.

Knowing that a high percentage of these students were 3-5 years behind grade level in reading, Dr. Davis recruited the appropriate high school student leaders to be reading tutors for the middle learning athletes. There were 10 students to a class, with 3-4 tutors. Each summer, each child averaged more than a grade year improvement.

Each child received a ribbon for completing each event. For many, these were the first awards of any kind they had ever won. The T-shirts were also very special and were worn throughout the year, with great pride. Many parents came out to cheer their children—many times at first. Every child received energetic cheering from hundreds of people—first or last.

Many of the children commented that this was the first time that they felt respect from accomplishing something—from peers and adults. Others reported that because their coach believed in them, they learned how to stay with it, learn, and achieve something.

Many of these kids have gone on to college, who surely wouldn't have considered it before the Teamworks program. Several got their start in the program, continued in high school and won college scholarships. At least one, Tonette Dyer, became a national class athlete at San Diego State University.

All because some lady wanted kids to enjoy running as she had.

Adelaide's Story

Fourth grader Adelaide had recently been adopted. Scars across her back and thighs testify to a dark period in her young life. She runs from a camera, fearful of what the photographer will require of her. Adelaide doesn't talk. In her past life, talking only got her into trouble. Adelaide joined Girls on the Run and I had the privilege to be her coach. Typically after most of our games we have a processing period afterward, during which each of the circle of 17 could say how a game related to some real life situation. Each day Adelaide would nervously shake her head, look to the ground and we would move on to the next girl in the circle. The first week, one of the other girls said fondly, "Oh, that's just Adelaide, she never talks."

Adelaide returned each week and communicated through her running: her moods, her feelings, her thoughts. When she was mad, her feet would slam the pavement, with a choppy stride, and blonde hair bouncing with each step. But when she was right with the world, for that one hour of her life, she would float across the asphalt, with feet lightly tapping the pavement, arms relaxed at her side and blonde hair flowing in a stream behind her.

On the last workout we ask the girls to say one or two words that would describe their Girls on the Run experience. Katherine said, "Cool!" Anna said, "Awesome." Takia said, "Crazy Fun." Adelaide paused, cleared her throat and said. . . nothing. She shook her head, looked to the ground and we continued. At the Girls on the Run Banquet, every girl receives her very own award, based on what makes each a special person. Katherine won the "smile with the red face" award. Anna was recognized for being "loyal to her friends." Takia was the "cool cat" winner. And Adelaide, won the "grand communicator" award—for communicating on a level that surpasses anything worldly: She let her body talk in the running motion, smiling.

When I called Adelaide up to receive her award—she came up and pulled a small card out of her back pocket. With a nod of her head she handed it to me and I opened it. Her face lit up, with a look that said "today is special."

I asked her if she would like to read what she wrote—and that brave little girl, closed her eyes tight, dug deep, and sweetly read her very own words to all of her friends in Girls on the Run and their families. "The word I wanted to say on the last day of Girls on the Run was 'Love'."

Adelaide took her voice back that day. Somewhere it had been lost or taken from her. But on this day, Adelaide shared with her friends the strength she had developed within, during the last 12 weeks.

From Molly Barker, Girls On The Run

Paul's Story

His name is Paul. He is 39 years old—a handsome professional man—Paul drives a BMW, wears custom suits with starched crisp white button-down shirts. He is respected and reserved. Yet little known to his friends is the hell in which he has lived. You see, eight years ago his wife—his life partner and best friend— died while giving birth to their daughter Shelby.

Paul's world suddenly changed. The high level executive position and a million dollar home were not as important as his dear daughter—who now looks like an average eight year old. But Shelby has the intellectual and conceptual understanding of a four year old. Shelby is often afraid to speak because some schoolmates make fun of her, call her dummy or generally disregard her as anything, but a nuisance. When the Girls on the Run (GOTR) brochure floated home in Shelby's book bag, Paul saw the possibilities and signed her up.

Shelby's spirit soared at girls on the run. Her teammates understood her uniqueness and accepted her not in spite of it—but because of it. As the days and weeks went by, Shelby came to trust her teammates. They weren't like the other girls at school. They wrapped their little souls around her and walked her through the Girls on the Run games and activities. They listened to her when she had something to say and they valued her for who she was.

Paul was at the finish line waiting for Shelby to finish her first GOTR 5K, applauding each finisher. One hour later every girl had finished, except one. While most folks had moved on to the after race party, the police escort came into view, and just ahead of it was a small figure with blond pigtails flopping. Even from a distance she appeared to be on a mission: arms pumping like pistons, her coaches beside her. Word spread that Shelby was finishing and the finish area filled up with hundreds of people. Stoically standing in the middle of the road, at the finish line was Paul: starched shirt— khaki pants and polished loafers, every hair in place. Shelby's jacket was neatly draped across his left arm.

As Shelby approached, Paul lost it. He dropped to his knees, lifted his arms and the tears flowed and flowed and he embraced her, celebrating the greatest victory of their lives together.

From Molly Barker, **Girls on the Run**

Alex

Alex is eight years old, and he has been going to the Youth Fitness Center for six months. Though he enjoyed playing team sports because of the camaraderie, Alex was not the athletic type. He didn't have much confidence in ever becoming a "sporty" guy, either. He didn't have much endurance on the soccer field or swimming laps, and when he was smaller, he had poor muscle tone. He was at risk of dropping out of exercise at a crucial time in his life, and was gaining weight.

At the YFC, Alex was challenged by his instructor, but was given the attention needed. While griping about the toughness of the workouts, he slowly improved his endurance, and began to enjoy the challenges. On many days he would not look forward to the session, but afterwards would excitedly brag about staying longer and longer on the treadmill or the stair machine.

The result: Alex is more confident about his strength, his body, and his overall outlook on life. He's also slimmed down and lost significant weight. He is showing significant increases in endurance activities and has better posture.

From Maria, about the YFC program for kids, out of the
Sarasota YMCA

SUCCESSFUL PROGRAMS

Most overweight or non-athletic kids believe that it is too late for them to start exercising. The research and the success stories overwhelmingly contradict this. The success of programs listed in the next section are due to the positive reinforcement of adults who want to help kids improve their lives.

Pamela Jackson was so upset by the death of a sibling that she started the *Youth Becoming Healthy Project*. She wanted others to avoid the suffering she experienced due to the premature death of her only brother due to complications from morbid obesity: www.ybhproject.org.

Across the world, teachers and youth organizations are creating fitness programs for kids. Leaders such as Coach Graves at Grace Presbyterian in Texas, or Kelly-Ann Way in Canada, show that one adult can make a big difference in the lives of kids. Force Youth Fitness in Greenville, S.C., and Fit4FunKidsFitness in Chicago are examples of organized programs open to communities (some with special needs). If there is not one in your community, look at the successful programs below, and start your own.

Students Run Los Angeles

This long running program challenges kids at risk in the Los Angeles area in September, to finish the L.A. Marathon in March. Their 95% success rate is impressive. More significant is the life-changing experience produced by the training and the finishing of the marathon. They have a continuous stream of success stories.

"Although the prospect of becoming an adult and managing all the requisite responsibilities is intimidating, I will face it head on thanks to knowledge I've gained through participation in Students Run L.A."

Tiffany, Chatsworth High School

SRLA mission statement
The mission of Students Run L.A. is to challenge at-risk secondary students to experience the benefits of goal-setting, character

development, adult mentoring and improved health by providing them with a truly life-changing experience: The training for and completion of The City of Los Angeles Marathon.

History and current program:

Students Run L.A. (SRLA) began as the brainchild of a Los Angeles Unified School District continuation high school teacher, who challenged a group of students to train with him to run the City of Los Angeles Marathon. The premise was simple: Take a group of young people whom many had written off as under-achievers, and help them accomplish something extraordinary. The program was immediately successful. Not only did it help students complete the marathon, it helped them graduate from high school. The program soon captured the attention of the Los Angeles Unified School District's Board of Education, which saw it as an effective and innovative dropout prevention and life skills program, and the school district became a sponsor of the program. In 1993, Students Run L.A. became an independent 501 (c) (3) organization.

Today, that one teacher and his handful of students have grown to 250 teachers and more than 2,000 students from more than 150 schools and community programs throughout Greater Los Angeles. The growth of the program has only increased its success. On average, more than 97% of SRLA students complete the marathon each year and more than 90% of the seniors who complete the marathon graduate from high school. (This compares with a graduation rate in the L.A. Unified School District of 65%.)

Even as it has grown, Students Run L.A. has remained a grass-roots, school-based program. Volunteer teachers/leaders at each school and community program organize running clubs, which range from a few to more than 100 students. They meet three to four times a week to run and to support each other in taking on this challenging goal. Leaders also take their students to monthly community races that bring together all 2,000-plus students. Students who are active in the program receive more than 500 hours of contact with these caring adult leaders during the season. During this time, students and leaders have a completely unique opportunity to spend time together and get to know one another. These casual hours spent together are often when students and their leaders have the best discussions about good nutrition, tobacco and drug use, peer pressure, and their outlooks on school and life.

Overview

Students Run L.A. is an innovative and exciting after-school intervention program for at-risk middle and high school students in the Greater Los Angeles Area. We provide a physical training and mentoring program to prepare more than 2,000 young people annually to complete the City of Los Angeles Marathon. As these students participate in our program and accomplish this seemingly impossible goal, they learn to set and achieve goals in other aspects of their lives.

Students Run L.A. fills a void in the lives of youth in the Greater Los Angeles Area and gives them better odds for success. After-school programs are not universally available to engage youth. The September 2001 report from Fight Crime: Invest in Kids California described a critical shortage of affordable after-school programs for middle school students in California, finding that "being unsupervised after school puts kids at greater risk of truancy, receiving poor grades, mental depression and substance abuse." Also, health issues abound. According to a 2002 study by the California Center for Public Health Advocacy that was based on data collected the year before, 26.5% of all children in California are overweight. The highest percentages of children who are overweight and physically inactive are found in Los Angeles County. SRLA strives to make an impact on the dim health prospects for teens facing high levels of life-threatening chronic diseases linked to poor nutrition, obesity and inactivity, including diabetes, heart disease, stroke and cancer. According to the Surgeon General, Type 2 diabetes, previously considered an adult disease, has increased dramatically in children and adolescents, many of whom are overweight.

SRLA provides a transformative wellness and self-improvement program, turning these statistics upside down and turning young lives around. This 14-year-old program uses the process of training for and completing a marathon to teach life lessons in goal-setting and discipline. SRLA challenges at-risk youngsters to do something that most people consider impossible — complete a marathon — and gives them the support and encouragement that they need to reach that goal. Through their participation, students build tremendous self-esteem and resiliency skills, which reduce their use of tobacco, alcohol and illegal drugs and improve their overall health.

Demographic profile of SRLA:
This year, more than 2,000 students are training with SRLA. The current population includes students 11 to 19 years old, with the majority being senior high school students 14 to 17. The students make up a diverse group: 52% are male, 48% are female; approximately 71% are Latino; 4% are African American; 9% are Asian; 12% are Anglo; and 4% are a combination of other ethnic backgrounds.

Impact on education:
One of the great benefits for students who participate in Students Run L.A. is the change that is apparent in their school work. The increase in self-esteem that comes from running progressively greater distances, coupled with the mentoring the students receive from their leaders, leads to better performance in school. As the students learn to set and complete short-term goals in each of their training runs, as a means to complete longer-term goals (the City of Los Angeles Marathon), they begin to understand how to apply themselves in the classroom in order to achieve the ultimate goal of graduation. Students have told us, "If I can finish a marathon, high school graduation will be a piece of cake!" SRLA has a graduation rate of more than 90%, as compared with the 65% rate for the Los Angeles Unified School District. Moreover, we know from our scholarship program that a significant number of our seniors continue their education after graduation.

Scholarship program:
One of the most important components of the Students Run L.A. experience is the scholarship program. This initiative provides scholarship awards to graduating seniors who have completed the marathon. The money may be used for participation in a program, class or activity that will promote their future educational goals. In addition, this program makes available mini-grants for younger students, who have completed the marathon, to apply to an educational experience, such as SAT preparation classes and enrichment courses. Students fill out an application describing themselves, their experience with SRLA, their experience in school, and their need for assistance. Applicants are evaluated on their grades, their essays, financial need, and the participation in the marathon. In Spring 2003, we awarded 48 scholarships and more than a dozen mini-grants.

More info: www.slra.org/about.html

Events

There are several events that work with school systems, local recreation programs, etc. to bring kids into the training process. Boogie the Bridge is a Canadian example. A "Tryathlon" has been successful in Australia (tryathlon.weetbix.com.au). The program that has reached the largest number of schools is associated with the Crim race in Flint, Mich. Be sure to read the section on this program below.

A growing number of other programs can be licensed or franchised in local areas. Here are some of them

Girls on the Run
The founder of Girls on the Run, Molly Barker, for example, says that the desired outcome "is NOT a reduction in weight, improvement in walking/running times or even an improvement in fitness levels. We measure success with the overall manner in

which the girls respect themselves and others....how they feel in their own skin."

At the end of a 12-week course, Molly's vision for each participant is the following:
1. Look others directly in the eye...feel good about who she is...and not judge others based on body-size, skin color or economic status.
2. Manage the turbulence of adolescence with the tools that she has acquired doing our program...for example: stands up to the peer pressure to perform unhealthy behaviors; knows exit strategies for bullying; can stop a gossip chain; can critically analyze messages she gets in the media about beauty and remains true to the concepts of who she is rather than conform to an unattainable stereotypical feminine standard;
3. Knows the importance of surrounding herself with people who are authentic, true, real...and lift each other up.
4. Knows that life isn't always "happy" and that true character is built during the challenges we confront when dealing with friends, losing the race, letting go of situations and people who are not good for us.
5. Believes that what she possesses on the inside....is beautiful, perfect, pure and all she needs to be a whole, thriving woman.

ABOUT GIRLS ON THE RUN INTERNATIONAL
The mission: To educate and prepare girls for a lifetime of self-respect and healthy living.

The program: Girls on the Run is a non-profit prevention program which uses an interactive curriculum and running to encourage preteen girls in developing self-respect and healthy lifestyles. Our curricula address all aspects of girls' development - their physical, emotional, mental, social and spiritual wellbeing. The lessons are aimed at providing girls the tools to avoid risky adolescent behaviors such as drug or alcohol use, early sexual activity and eating disorders/obesity.

Demographics:
- Girls on the Run Program: pre-teen girls ages 8-11 years and their families
- Girls on Track Program: girls ages 12-14 years and their families
- Program Facilitators/Coaches: women of all ages and their families

The growth of Girls on the Run, International:
- Founded in 1996 by four-time Hawaii Ironman triathlete, teacher & counselor Molly Barker
- Headquartered in Charlotte, N.C., with member councils in over 100 communities across the United States and Canada
- Growth Rate: From three councils in 1998 to 115 councils at the beginning of 2006; from 200 participants in 1998 to over 18,000 in 2005; over 50,000 girls have completed the program since 1996
- Recognized on NBC News and in O, the Oprah Magazine, PEOPLE, Better Homes & Gardens, Runner's World, Running Times, Cooking Light, Walking Magazine, Parent Magazine, American Girl Magazine, Healthy Kids Magazine, Daughter's Newsletter, ESPN, and local newspapers all over the country; Molly Barker's book Girls on Track: A Parent's Guide to Inspiring Our Daughters was published by Ballentine books in March, 2004
- Molly Barker was named "One of America's Most Inspirational Women" by Runner's World and featured in the ESPN Special "Apple Pie – Raising Champions" (along with Drew Bledsoe, Kenny Lofton, Mia Hamm, Grant Hill and others); she will be involved in the 2004 Oprah Hi, Gorgeous Tour as an expert in inspiring women and girls.

Program design:
- Our three 24-lesson curricula teach life skills through running games and workouts. The curricula are based on extensive educational research and "on-the-track" testing of lessons.
- The three-part curriculum is taught by certified Girls on the Run coaches and covers: Who am I? What are my values? What are my goals? Team Building: What does it mean to be supportive and supported? Finding My Place and My Voice in the Community

- Girls choose and conduct a community service project
- At each season's conclusion, girls have a chance to complete a 3.1 mile community running event with their "team"

Results to date:
- Academic evaluation of the program by Dr. Rita DiGioacchino DeBate (University of North Carolina Charlotte; Dept. Health Behavior and Administration) shows a "statistically significant" improvement in body image, eating attitudes and self-esteem
- Anecdotal evidence also indicates an improved sense of identity and an increasingly active lifestyle for program participants

The funding- Girls on the Run International partners with New Balance, Kellogg's Frosted Flakes and Goody's Hair Products and is supported by grants, donations and fees. Girls on the Run councils partner with or are not-for-profit 501(c)(3) organization; they are funded by corporate sponsorship, by donations, by private, state and federal grants. Fees are charged for the program, but sliding fee scales and scholarships make the program available to all who are interested.

Partnerships-GOTR councils partner with a variety of nonprofit organizations including community hospitals; recreation centers; public and private schools; YMCA's; Boys & Girls Clubs; health departments; law enforcement organizations; running & fitness clubs; and universities; many establish their own independent 501(c)(3) organizations.

Council locations: Arizona, Arkansas, California, Colorado, Connecticut, Delaware, Florida, Georgia, Idaho, Illinois, Indiana, Kentucky, Maine, Maryland, Massachusetts, Michigan, Minnesota, Missouri, Nebraska, New Hampshire, New Jersey, New York, North Carolina, Ohio, Oregon, Pennsylvania, South Carolina, Tennessee, Texas, Vermont, Virginia, Washington, Washington DC, Wisconsin and Canada

For more information: Check out our web site at www.girlsontherun.org or contact the national office via email at info@girlsontherun.org or call 800-901-9965

MARATHON KIDS

Marathon Kids® is a ten-year-old non-profit organization. It's a resonating, wildly popular, free running/walking and nutrition program for K-5th graders and their parents. The children usually do the program through public, private or home schools. It is in Austin, Dallas, Houston, and Texas Rio Grande Valley. In 06-07, we are launching in Los Angeles and Baltimore...and perhaps more cities.

The children complete a 26.2 mile running log and a 26.2 day

There are 100,000 little Marathon Kids this year who are doing the free six month program. The children earn rewards. There is nothing they can buy. There is a big Kick Off and then later a Final Mile Medal Celebration. Part of the mission of Marathon Kids is to "wrap community" around these children and also, through donated university track and field stadiums, allow the children the experience of being on a college campus.

The children acquire the love and habit of running. They also acquire the habit of making healthy food choices. They are challenged to eat 26.2 days a month of 5-a-day fruits and veggies. In the summer, they have 26.2 challenges of movement...and 26.2 recipes for summer healthy eating to complete!

Olympians, community runners, school teachers, police officers, college athletes, Governors, Mayors...all join in with Marathon Kids. It is a six month "love-in" for little ones. We "throw the net wide," trying to capture the imagination of the boy or girl who would usually never ever raise his/her hand, thinking "this is something I can do." We do not target the over-achievers or "soccer mom kids." We customize the free program for those who most need the encouragement and the empowerment of being a Marathon Kid.

For more information:
www.MarathonKids.com

Crim Festival of Races, Flint, Mich.
Youth Fun and Fitness Program

Of all of the kids programs that are associated with events, this program is the best that I've seen in operation. Over 10,000 kids participate every year in Flint, Mich. There are 38 schools that conduct the curriculum from September through June. There are also 20 youth clubs that were organized during the summer months, using the Crim training guidelines. They have three goal events for kids: Crim Kids, Kid's Classic, and Teddy Bear Trot. This program has changed the fitness and the quality of life in a major way for kids and families in this community.

- Educate youth on the importance of regular exercise
- Educate youth on the importance of healthy eating
- Educate youth about the negative effects of substance abuse
- Train and prepare youth of an age appropriate run/walk event

By the end of 8 weeks
1. Each participant will train to complete the following age appropriate run/walk course
   Ages 3-8: one quarter mile
   Ages 9-12: one quarter mile, 1 mile or 5K
   Ages 13-15: 1 mile, 5K or 8K
   Ages 16-18: 5K, 8K, or 10 mile

Note consider each child's ability, physical disabilities and/or health issues when choosing a race distance

2. Each participant should be able to express the importance of regular physical activity
3. Each participant should be able to name at least one health risk related to substance abuse

Director: Marti Austin

Stretch-n-Grow is a comprehensive fitness program for kids. We are committed to helping educators and parents establish a foundation of exercise and proper nutrition at an early age, before habits gel. *The Stretch-n-Grow* program teaches children the fundamentals of a healthy lifestyle. With weekly emphasis on exercise and good food choices, our extensive curriculum covers virtually every wellness issue...self-esteem, safety, hygiene, and environmental issues are just a few examples of our discussion topics. Classes are taught at child care centers by *Stretch-n-Grow* coaches who make exercising, "EXERciting!!"

The mission of Stretch-n-Grow is:
- To teach as many children as possible the basics of proper exercise, nutrition, and related health issues.
- To establish patterns and a positive attitude at an early age that will be the foundation for a continuing physical conditioning program and good heath.
- To prepare children for participation in physical education and athletic programs.
- To provide parents, caregivers and educators of young children with current information concerning proper exercise and nutrition, and other related issues in an effort to encourage each family to participate together in a fitness program.

As of January 2006, there were 245 franchises in 37 states and 11 countries. The countries that have a Stretch-n-Grow program are as follows: United States, Ireland, Australia, United Kingdom, Canada, New Zealand, Hong Kong, Guatemala, Portugal, Puerto Rico, and Spain.

Also, as of January 2006, there were over 80,000 children participating in Stretch-n-Grow each week worldwide. And, this number increases weekly!

For more information about Stretch-n-Grow or if you are interested in bringing the Stretch-n-Grow program to your school, child care center, or gym, please contact Cherie Behrens owner of Stretch-n-Grow of Central/North Charlotte at 704-277-2327 or *cbehrens@stretch-n-grow.com.*

It's never too early to start a strong foundation for a lifetime of exercise and fitness habits that will result in good health, strength and positive attitudes.

Also look for a book with activities and concepts: The Treasure of Health and Happiness

Kidsrunning.com has several books with great program suggestions:
Happy Feet, Healthy Food, Your Child's First Journal of Exercise and Healthy Eating, The Treasure of Health and Happiness.

JUST RUN
In coordination with the Big Sur International Marathon

JUST RUN Monterey County is a FREE program funded by the Big Sur International Marathon and private donations. The goal is to promote fitness and healthy lifestyles in the second to eighth grades. The JUST RUN program has many aspects including:

1. JUST RUN across the United States – implementing non-competitive and competitive group running programs in the schools, either during or after school, with the assistance of teachers or parent volunteers. This provides a program that teaches activity, fitness principles, goal setting, fun, stretching, and physical development.
2. The website *www.justrun.org* provides a focal point for students and volunteers to record their accumulated mileage in an imaginary run mapped across the United States. In addition to providing incentive for your group, this context can be used as a history or geography lesson to study locations that your school passes through on your way across the United States. You can see an example of the main screen for the program,

showing the total number of children enrolled, the number of JUST DEEDS earned, and the total number of miles run. The next screen shows the page for a child and his school, listing the total number of JUST DEEDS and miles run for the whole school, and also for that individual child. Children who reach certain milestones for Deeds and miles run earn a T-shirt, as this child did. You can also see the path across the United States, with their current position marked by the Just Run shoe in the vicinity of New York City. The next screen shows the links to all the points the children in the school have passed on their journey. The last screen shows the JUST DEEDS log and running log for this child, Connor.

3. The website will also provide fitness tips for students and volunteer leaders, diet and nutrition advice, local events and activities for students, a downloadable running log, and a way to compare your school or groups' progress with others in the program.

4. JUST DEEDS - in conjunction with running and physical activity, the program will promote good citizenship and good deeds. Incentive awards will be provided as students accumulate mileage totals up to the marathon distance of 26 miles while performing 26 good citizenship deeds.

5. TEAM USA Monterey Bay's elite runners, coach, and local runners will provide clinics and demonstrations at your school as well as larger youth running clinics, both during the school year and in the Summer. This will also include training the leaders and volunteers at each school.

6. JUST RACE – The Big Sur International Marathon already provides funds to schools based on school participation in the 5K run on marathon day in late April. The marathon is actively working with other local race directors to add fun runs and races for children to each local adult race and to establish separate children only races and fun runs.

7. JUST RUN FROM DRUGS – the program will emphasize a drug free and healthy active lifestyle.

8. HELP – the JUST RUN program will work actively to support the new initiative in Monterey County called HELP (Healthy

Eating Lifestyle Principals) to work for healthy fruit and vegetables in school lunch programs as well as an increased role for physical activity.

9. JUST WALK OR ROLL – the JUST RUN program will include children with disabilities or those who want to accumulate mileage and be active by walking or who are wheel chair bound.

10 JUST RUN WITH YOUR PARENTS – There will be incentives in the program for children who run with their parents in order to promote family fitness.

11. GRANTS or FINANCIAL ASSISTANCE for children who need running shoes or clothes, teachers working after hours, or other fitness related activity programs may be possible.

12. IF YOU ARE OUTSIDE OF MONTEREY COUNTY and are interested in this program we can provide use of the website and shirt logo and program materials at a small franchise fee. Call Sally Smith at the marathon office at 831-625-6226 for information.

When a school chooses to do the JUST RUN program they receive the following from the Big Sur International Marathon Just Run program:

1. Access to the comprehensive JUST RUN website *(www.justrun. org)* with information for children, parents, teachers and group leaders on leading an active lifestyle and eating properly.

2. A school visit and orientation presentation to the children and group leaders from JUST RUN program personnel and elite runners from the Big Sur Distance Project.

3. Incentive awards for mileage accumulated by running and walking including plastic shoes, 5, 10, 15, 20, 25 mile tokens, wrist bracelets for 26, 50, 75, and 100.

4. Shirt awards for those accumulating 26 miles of activity and doing 26 "Just Deeds," which are acts of good citizenship or good deeds.

5. Training session for leaders in website use and implementation of the program.

6. Online and phone advice.

7. A password to the JUST RUN across the USA program for accumulating group mileage in a virtual run across the USA.

8.   Colorful JUST RUN posters for each classroom.
9.   JUST RUN brochures explaining the program.
10. JUST RUN hats for the group leaders.
11. U.S.A. Track and Field Association "Be a Champion" colorful Postcards and the "Be a Champion" pledge for each child.
12. Follow up elite athlete visit to present incentive awards.

New York Road Runners Club Foundation
Offers goals setting, nutritional and academic components for 15,000 kids, in over 100 schools and communitiy centers.

Greater Clarkesburg (WVA) 10K
Has a training program offered to kids in the area as a preparation for a one mile race. Kids will run one mile at a time, accumulating 25 miles during the months leading up to the race weekend. There are rewards given during the training for each 5 miles logged in – given by local merchants.

Websites:

Information
www.Kidsrunning.com
Note: Carol Goodrow has lots of helpful material—and great books
www.fitnessforyouth.umich.edu
www.fitnessmba.com
www.kidzworld.com
www.acefitness.org/ofk/youthfitness
www.cdc.gov/verb
www.KidsHealth.org
www.fitnessfinders.net

Games and activities
www.kidsrunning.com
www.pecentral.com
www.runnersworld.com

Some programs in the Los Angeles area:
Healthy Eating Lifestyle Program (Harbor UCLA) (310) 222-8241
Health Care Partners (310) 214-0811 ext 5070
Power Play (310) 289-8242, (323) 937-7811
Kids Shape (888) 600-6444

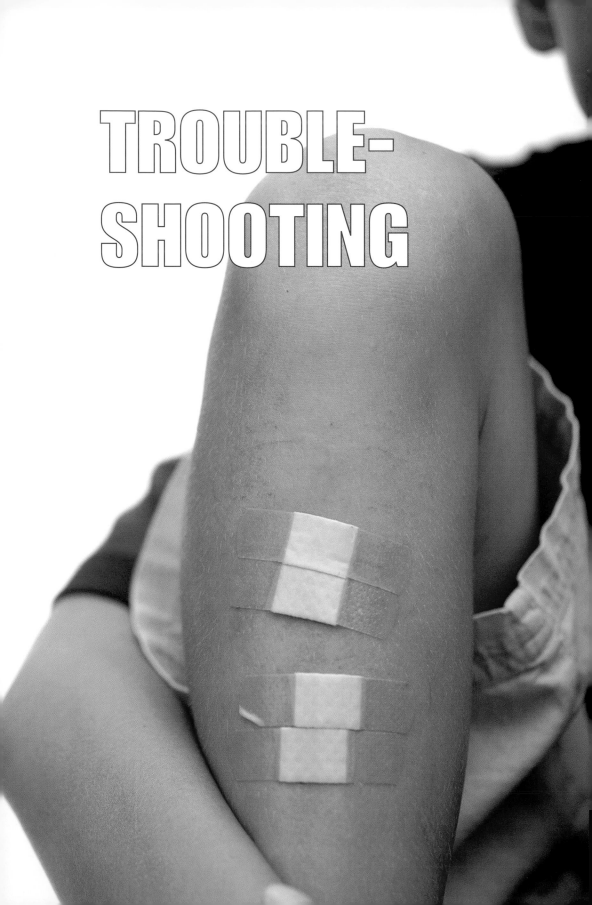

TROUBLE-
SHOOTING

- Side pain
- It hurts!
- No energy…
- I feel great one day—but the next day…
- No motivation
- Cramps in the muscles
- Upset stomach or diarrhea
- How do I start back when I've had time off?
- Headache
- Should I run when I have a cold?
- Street safety
- Dogs
- Strechting & strengthening
- Your journal—for planing, evalutation and motivation
- Troubleshooting aches & pains

Side Pain

This is very common, and usually has a simple fix. Normally it is not anything to worry about…it just hurts. This condition is due to 1) the lack of deep breathing, and 2) going a little too fast from the beginning of the exercise. You can correct #2 easily by walking more at the beginning, and slowing down your workout pace. Kids almost always start too fast, and then fail to deep-breathe.

Deep breathing from the beginning of a run can prevent side pain. This way of inhaling air is performed by diverting the air you breathe into your lower lungs. Also called "belly breathing," this is how we breathe when asleep, and it provides maximum opportunity for oxygen absorption. If you don't deep breathe from the beginning of your exercise, you're not getting the oxygen you need. The side pain will tell you. By slowing down, walking, and breathing deeply for a while, the pain may go away. But sometimes it does not. Most runners just continue to run and walk with the side pain. In 50 years of running and helping others run, I've not seen any lasting negative effect from those who run with a side pain.

You don't have to take in a maximum breath to perform this technique. Simply breathe a normal breath but send it to the lower lungs. You know that you have done this if your stomach goes up and down as you inhale and exhale. If your chest goes up and down, you are breathing shallowly.

Note: never breathe in and out rapidly. This can lead to hyperventilation, dizziness, and fainting.

It Hurts!

Is it just a passing ache, or a real injury?

Most of the aches and pains you feel during and after exercise will go away within a few minutes. If the pain occurs when running, just walk for an additional two minutes, jog a few strides, and walk another two minutes. If the pain comes back after doing this four or five times, stop running and walk. If the pain goes away when you walk, just walk for the rest of the workout.

Walking pain

When the pain stays around when walking, try a very short stride. Walk for a 30-60 seconds. If it still hurts when walking, try sitting down, and massaging the area that hurts, if you can. Sit for two to four minutes. When you try again to walk, and it still hurts, call it a day—your workout is over.

It's an injury if....

There's inflammation—swelling in the area

There's loss of function—the foot, knee, etc. doesn't work correctly

There's pain—it hurts and keeps hurting or gets worse

Treatment suggestions:

1. See a doctor who has treated other runners successfully and wants to get you back on the road or trail.
2. Take 2-5 days off from any activity that could irritate it, to get the healing started, more if needed.
3. If the area is next to the skin (tendon, foot, etc), rub a chunk of ice on the area(s)—constantly rubbing for 15 min until the area gets numb. Continue to do this for a week after you feel no symptoms. Ice bags and gel ice do no good at all in most cases.
4. If the problem is inside a joint or muscle, call your doctor and ask if you can use prescription strength anti-inflammatory medication. Don't take any medication without a doctor's advice—and follow that advice.
5. If this is a muscle injury, see a veteran sports massage therapist. Try to find one who has a lot of successful experience treating the injured area. Magic fingers and hands can often work wonders.

This is advice from one runner to another. For more info on injuries, treatment, etc., see the injury section of this book, *Year Round Plan* and *Galloway's Book On Running Second Edition*.

No Energy Today

There will be a number of days each year when you will not feel like exercising. On most of these, you can turn it around and feel great. Occasionally, you will not be able to do this, because of an infection, lingering fatigue, or other physical problems. Here's a list of things that can give you energy. If these actions don't help you energize yourself, then read the nutrition sections—particularly the blood sugar chapter in this book—or in *Galloway's Book on Running Second Edition.*

1. Low blood sugar is a common reason for lack of motivation, and low energy. Eat an energy bar, with water or (better) caffeinated beverage, about an hour before the run. Read the chapter in this book on this issue.

2. Instead of #1, half an hour before exercising, you could drink 100-200 calories of a sports drink that has a mix of 80% simple carbohydrate and 20% protein. The product Accelerade has this already put together.

3. Just walk for five minutes away from your house, office, etc., and the energy often kicks in. Forward movement gets the attitude moving too. Many kids just have to get into a run with other kids, and they are suddenly motivated.

4. One of the prime reasons for no energy is that you didn't re-load within 30 minutes after your last exercise session: 100-200 calories of a mix that is 80% simple carbohydrate and 20% protein (**Endurox** R4 is the product that has this formulated).

5. Low-carb diets will result in low energy to get motivated before a workout, and often no energy to finish the workout.

5. In most cases it is fine to keep going even if you aren't energetic. But if you sense an infection, see a doctor. If the low energy stays around for several days, see a nutritionist that knows about the special needs of exercisers and/or get some blood work done. This may be due to inadequate iron, B vitamins, energy stores, etc.

Note: if you have any problems with caffeine, don't consume any products containing it. As always, if you sense any health problem, see a doctor.

I Feel Great One Day...But Not the Next

It helps for you to tell the kids that you have days like this also. There are a few common reasons for this, but there will always be "those days" when the body doesn't seem to work right, or the gravity seems heavier than normal—and you cannot find a reason.

1. Pushing through. In most cases, this is a one-day occurrence. Most runners just put more walking into the mix, and get through it. Before pushing, however, make sure that you don't have a medical reason why you feel bad.

2. Heat and/or humidity will make you feel worse. You will often feel great when the temperature is below 60F and miserable when 75F or above.

3. Low blood sugar can make any run a bad run. You may feel good at the start and suddenly feel like you have no energy. Every step seems to take a major effort. Read the chapter in this book about this topic.
4. Low motivation. Use the rehearsal techniques in the motivation/mental toughness section of this book. This has helped numerous runners turn their minds around—even in the middle of a run.
5. Infection can leave you feeling lethargic, achy, and unable to run at the same pace that was easy a few days earlier. The effects of infection can last for weeks, leaving you lethargic during exercise, when energy is fine during the other activities in life. Check the normal signs (fever, chills, swollen lymph glands, etc.) and at least call your doctor if you suspect something.
6. Medication and alcohol, even when taken the day before, can leave a hangover that dampens a workout.
7. A slower start can make the difference between a good day and a bad day. When your body is on the edge of fatigue or other stress, it only takes a few seconds too fast per mile, walking and/or running, to push into discomfort or worse.

Cramps in the Muscles

At some point, most people who run experience cramps. These muscle contractions usually occur in the feet or the calf muscles and may come during a run or walk, or they may hit at random. Most commonly, they will occur at night, or when you are sitting around at your desk or watching TV in the afternoon or evening.

Cramps vary in severity. Most are mild but some can grab so hard that they shut down the muscles and hurt when they seize up. Massage and a short and gentle movement of the muscle can help to bring most of the cramps around. Odds are that stretching will make the cramp worse, or tear the muscle fibers.

Most cramps are due to overuse—doing more than in the recent past, or continuing to put yourself at your limit, especially in warm weather. Look at the pace and distance of your runs and walks in your training journal to see if you have been running too far, or too fast, or both.

Heavier runners and older runners will tend to experience a quicker increase in cramps than others when the temperature rises above 60°F. Remember to slow down by 30 sec a mile for every five degrees above 60°F.

- Continuous running increases cramping. Taking walk breaks more often can reduce or eliminate cramps. Those who experience cramps when they run at a ratio of 4-1 will often eliminate them with a 2-1 or 3-1. Several runners who used to cramp when they ran a minute and walked a minute, stopped cramping with a ratio of run 30 seconds and walk 30-60 seconds—even when running at the same pace. Be sure to explain to the kids that you can't wait until the cramps appear to take walk breaks. By taking the walks from the beginning you keep pushing back the threshold of fatigue and cramping.
- During hot weather, a good electrolyte beverage can help to replace the salts that your body loses in sweating (consumed throughout the day, not during a workout). A drink like Accelerade, for example, can help to top off these minerals by drinking 6-8 oz every 1-2 hours. Keep a pitcher in the refrigerator.
- On very long hikes, walks or runs, however, the continuous sweating, especially when drinking a lot of fluid, can push your sodium levels too low and produce muscle cramping. If this happens regularly, a buffered salt tablet has helped greatly: Succeed.
- Many medications, especially those designed to lower cholesterol, have muscle cramps as one of their known side effects. Runners who use medications and cramp should ask their doctor if there are alternatives. Kids that are on medications, and are experiencing cramps, should have this checked out.

Here are several ways of dealing with cramps:

1. Take a longer and gentler warm-up.
2. Shorten your run segment.
3. Start each workout more slowly.
4. Slow down your walk, and walk more.
5. Shorten your distance on a hot/humid day.
6. Break your run up into two segments.
7. Look at any other exercise that could be causing the cramps.
8. Take a buffered salt tablet at the beginning of your exercise.

Note: if you have high blood pressure, ask your doctor before taking any salt product.

Upset Stomach or Diarrhea

Sooner or later, virtually every runner has at least one episode with nausea or diarrhea. It comes from the buildup of total stress that you accumulate. Most commonly, it is the stress of running on that day, due to the causes listed below. But stress is the result of many unique conditions within the individual. Your body triggers the nausea/diarrhea to get you to reduce the exercise, which will reduce the stress. Here are the common causes.

1. **Exercising too hard or too long** is the most common cause. Runners are confused about this, because the pace doesn't feel too fast in the beginning. Each person has a level of fatigue that triggers these conditions. Slowing down (and taking more walk breaks) will help you manage the problem.

2. **Eating too much or too soon before the run.** Your system has to work hard running, and works hard to digest food. Doing both at the same time raises stress and results in nausea, etc. Having food in your stomach, in the process of being digested, is an extra stress and a likely target for elimination.

3. **Eating a high fat or high protein diet.** Even one meal that has over 50% of the calories in fat or protein can lead to nausea/diarrhea (N/D) hours later. Explain to kids that the foods they eat for lunch, the quantity, and the snacks afterward can produce these conditions.

4. **Eating too much the afternoon or evening, the day before.** A big evening meal will still be in the gut the next morning, being digested. When you bounce up and down on a run, which you will, you add stress to the system and results in N/D.

5. **Heat and humidity** are a major cause of these problems. Explain to the kids that each of us is affected differently. Some people don't adapt to heat well and experience N/D with minimal buildup of temperature or humidity. But in hot conditions, everyone has a core body temperature increase that will result in significant stress to the system—often causing nausea, and sometimes diarrhea. By slowing down, taking more walk breaks, and pouring water over your head, you can manage this better.

6. **Drinking too much water before a run.** If you have too much water in your stomach, and you are bouncing around, you put stress on the digestive system. Reduce your intake to the bare minimum. Most exercisers don't need to drink any fluid before a run that is 60 minutes or less.

7. **Drinking too much of a sugar/electrolyte drink.** Water is the easiest substance for the body to process. The addition of sugar and/or electrolyte minerals, as in a sports drink, makes the substance harder to digest. During a workout (especially on a hot day), it is best to drink only water. Cold water is best.

8. **Drinking too much fluid too soon after a workout.** Kids are prime offenders in this case. Even if you are very thirsty, don't gulp down large quantities of any fluid. Try to drink no more than 6-8 oz, every 20 minutes or so. If you are particularly prone to this N/D, just take 2-4 sips, every five minutes or so. When the body is very

stressed and tired, it's not a good idea to consume a sugar drink. The extra stress of digesting the sugar can lead to problems.

9. **Don't let running be stressful to you.** Some kids get too obsessed about getting their exercise—or keeping up with kids that are currently in better shape. This adds stress. Relax and let your run diffuse some of the other tensions in your life.

How Do I Start Back, when I've Had Time Off?

The longer you've been away from running, the slower you must return. I want to warn you now that you will reach a point when you feel totally back in shape—but you are not. Children need to be reminded that they must start back slowly when they had had time off from illness, vacation, injury, etc. Stay with the plan below for a virtually painless return to fitness. But when in doubt, be more conservative. Remember that you want kids (and adults) to be in this for the long run!

Less than 2 weeks off: You will feel like you are starting over again, but should come back quickly. Start back like a beginner for the first week. If all is well, with no aches and pains, the second and third week back could see a transition into the schedule you were using before you had your layoff.

14 days to 29 days off: You will also feel like you are starting over again, and it will take longer to get it all back: Within about 4-5 weeks you should be back to normal. Start as a beginner, for the first two weeks. If all goes well, use the next three weeks to transition back into the exercise that was planned for that time period.

More than one month off: If you have not run for a month or more, start over again, like a beginner. Use one of the three schedules in my book *Getting Started, Galloway's Book on Running,* or *Year Round Plan*. You'll be exercising every other day, starting with two segments of five minutes each, with a rest break between. You could add 2-3 minutes of exercise, each session, as you build back.

Headache

There are several reasons why exercisers, and especially runners, get headaches. While uncommon, they happen to the average exerciser about 1-5 times a year. The extra stress that exercise puts on the body is normally not a problem, but can be just too much for your system when there is other stress. Many runners find that a dose of an over-the-counter headache medication takes care of the problem. As always, consult with your doctor about use of medication. Here are the causes/solutions.

Dehydration—if you run in the morning, make sure that you hydrate well the day before. Adults find that alcohol the night before can produce a morning exercise headache. Also watch the salt in your dinner meal the night before. A good sports drink like Accelerade, taken throughout the day the day before, will help to keep your fluid levels and your electrolytes "topped off." If you exercise in the afternoon, follow the same advice leading up to your run, on the day of the run.

Medications can often produce dehydration—There are some medications that make exercisers more prone to headaches. Check with your doctor.

Too hot for you—exercise at a cooler time of the day (usually in the morning before the sun gets above the horizon). On a hot day, pour water over your head. When running, slow down pace as the temperature increases: 30 sec a mile slower for every five degrees above 60°F.

Starting a little too fast—start all workouts more slowly. When running, walk more during the first half of the run.

Running further than you have run in the recent past—monitor your mileage and don't increase more than about 15% further than you have run on any single run in the past week.

Low blood sugar level—Be sure that you boost your BLS with a snack, about 30-60 min before you exercise. If you are used to having it, caffeine in a beverage can sometimes help this situation also.

If prone to migraines—generally avoid caffeine, and try your best to avoid dehydration. Talk to your doctor about other possibilities.

Watch your neck and lower back—If you have a slight forward lean as you run, you can put pressure on the spine—particularly in the neck and lower back. Read the form chapter in this book and run upright.

Should I Run when I Have a Cold?

There are so many individual health issues with a cold that you must talk with a doctor before you exercise when you have an infection. Parents need to talk with the doctor about whether an infection should result in no exercise.

Lung infection—don't run! A virus in the lungs can move into the heart and kill you. Lung infections are usually indicated by coughing. If you even suspect a lung infection, don't exercise.

Common cold? There are many infections that initially seem to be a normal cold but are not. At least call your doctor's office to get clearance before exercising. Be sure to explain how long and how intense you plan to exercise, and what, if any, medication you are taking.

Throat infection and above—most exercisers will be given the OK, but check with the doc.

Street Safety

Each year several runners are hit by cars when running. Most of these are preventable. Here are the primary reasons and what you can do about them:

1. The driver is intoxicated or preoccupied by cell phone, etc.

Always be on guard—even when running on the sidewalk or pedestrian trail. Many of the fatal crashes occurred when the driver lost control of the car, and came up behind the runner, on the wrong side of the road. I know it is wonderful to be on "cruise control" in your right brain, but you can avoid a life threatening situation if you will just keep looking around, and anticipate.

2. The runner dashes across an intersection against the traffic light.

When running or walking with another person, don't try to follow blindly across an intersection. Runners who quickly sprint across the street without looking are often surprised by cars coming from unexpected directions. The best rule is the one that you heard as a child: When you get to an intersection, stop, see what the traffic situation is. Look both ways, and look both ways again (and again) before crossing. Have an option to bail out of the crossing if a car surprises you from any direction.

3. Sometimes, runners wander out into the street as they talk and run—Kids do this often!

One of the very positive aspects of running becomes a negative one, in this case. Yes, chat and enjoy time with your friends. But every runner in a group needs to be responsible for his or her own safety, footing, etc. The biggest mistake I see is that the runners at the back of a group assume that they don't have to be concerned about traffic at all. This lack of concern is a very risky situation.

In general, be ready to save yourself from a variety of traffic problems by following the rules below and any other that apply to specific situations. Even though the rules below seem obvious, many runners get hit by cars each year by ignoring them. Go over these rules with kids regularly.

- Be constantly aware of vehicular traffic, at all times.
- Assume that all drivers are drunk or crazy or both. When you see a strange movement by a car, be ready to get out of the way.
- Mentally practice running for safety. Get into the practice of

thinking ahead at all times, with a plan for that current stretch of road.

- Run/walk as far off the road as you can. If possible run on a sidewalk or pedestrian trail.
- Run/walk facing traffic. A high percentage of traffic deaths come from those who run with the flow of traffic, and do not see the threat from behind.
- Wear reflective gear at night. I've heard the accounts and this apparel has saved lives.
- Take control over your safety—you are the only one on the road who will usually save yourself.

Dogs

When you enter a dog's territory, you may be in for a confrontation. Here are my suggestions for dealing with your "dog days":

1. There are several good devices that will help deter dogs: an old fashioned stick, rocks, pepper spray, and some electronic signal devices. If you are in a new area, or an area of known dogs, I recommend that you have one of these at all times.
2. At the first sign of a dog ahead, or barking, try to figure out where the dog is located, whether the dog is a real threat, and what territory the dog is guarding.
3. The best option is to run/walk a different route.
4. If you really want or need to run past the dog, pick up a rock if you don't have another anti-dog device.
5. Watch the tail. If the tail does not wag, beware.
6. As you approach the dog, it is natural for the dog to bark and head toward you. Raise your rock as if you will throw it at the dog. In my experience, the dog withdraws about 90% of the time. You may need to do this several times before getting through the dog's territory. Keep your arms up.
7. In a few cases you will need to throw the rock, and sometimes another if the dog keeps coming.
8. In less that 1% of the hundreds of dog confrontations I've had, there is something wrong with the dog, and it continues to move

toward you. Usually the hair will be up on the dog's back. Try to find a barrier to get behind, yell loudly in hopes that the owner or someone will help you. If a car comes by, try to flag down the driver, and either stay behind the car as you get out of the dog's territory, or get in the car for protection if that is appropriate.

9. Develop your own voice. Some use a deep commanding voice and some use a high-pitched voice. Whichever you use, exude confidence and command.

Stretching

I believe that most runners will incur significant injury risk if they stretch regularly. Therefore, I don't recommend stretching for walking and running particularly. Beware of stretching out muscles that have tightened up due to exertion. Stretching a fatigued muscle can injure it significantly—during one stretch. Massage (even when using a tool like "the stick") can help a tired muscle recover and reduce the tightness.

Strengthening

I don't see any benefit in doing leg strengthening for walking and running. Hill training, as described in *Galloway's book on Running 2nd ed, & Testing Yourself* can strengthen the legs for running more effectively, according to my experience.

Foot strengthening: "the foot squincher"

I believe that this exercise can reduce the chance of plantar fasciia and other foot injuries. Point your toes downward and contract the muscles in each foot, one at a time. Stop each "squinch" when the foot cramps. Do this throughout the day, 15-30 times.

Postural muscle exercises

"Arm running" can reduce shoulder fatigue, as it strengthens the muscles that maintain the upper body in the upright position. While standing, with hand-held weights, move the arms through a slightly exaggerated motion you would use when running. Pick a weight that would allow you to do sets of 10, without straining on the last two or three.

"The crunch" is performed while lying on your back, knees bent. Raise your head and shoulders slightly off the floor and back down and up—so that you never rest the stomach muscles. Tilt the upper body slightly on one side and then the other to strengthen a range of abdominal and trunk muscle groups.

YOUR JOURNAL —For Planning, Evaluation, and Motivation

This is your book

This can be the first writing experience for many kids. Explain that by filling out their journal, they are actually writing a book, which may include areas other than exercise. Whether you want to improve or not, the journal helps you get organized in advance and then collect the details for evaluation. If we don't record the data and then look for the reasons behind our problems, we will have a tendency to repeat them.

Computer logs, training journals, notebooks

There are a growing number of software products that allow you to sort through information more quickly. In working with a company (PC Coach) to incorporate my training program, I discovered that this format speeds up the search for needed information. As you set up your own codes and sections you can pick data that is important to you, sort it to see trends, and plan ahead. Some software (including mine) allows you to download data from a heart monitor or GPS watch.

Most exercisers use notebook products. My *Galloway's Training Journal* has 52 weeks of entries with spaces for the key data items I've found significant. Simple log books can be made from school notebooks or calendars. The best product is one that you will use regularly.

The planning process

1. Look over your chosen schedule from *Testing Yourself, Marathon, Year Round Plan, Galloway's Book On Running Second Edition,* and *Half Marathon.*
2. Write down the key workouts and major events, on the appropriate weeks in your journal. Take a hi-lighter, etc., to make these weeks stand out.
3. Write down the assigned workouts, for each day of each week for the next eight weeks—in pencil.

4. Look at each of the next eight weeks quickly to make sure you don't have any conflicts that require adjusting the workouts.
5. Each week, add another week's workouts in pencil, and note any changes in your travel, etc., schedule.
6. Each week, look ahead carefully at the next two weeks to ensure that the workouts are adjusted to your family's real life schedule.

The data recording

As soon as you can after exercise, write the results in your journal:
- Mileage or # of steps
- Pace
- Types of exercise
- Rest minutes (when standing around, etc)
- Aches or pains
- Problems

In addition, you may also record:

Time of exercise:
- Total Time spent
- Weather
- Temperature
- Precipitation
- Humidity
- Walk-Run frequency
- Any special segments (speed, hills, race, etc.)
- Running companion
- Terrain
- How did you feel (1-10)
- Comments

2. Go back over the list again and fill in more details—emotional responses, changes in energy or blood sugar level, and location of places where you had aches and pains—even if they went away after a while. You are looking for patterns of items that could indicate injury, blood sugar problems, lingering fatigue, etc.

Your morning pulse can help you monitor over-training

Recording Morning Pulse—immediately upon waking
1. As soon as you are conscious—but before you have thought much about anything—count your pulse rate for a minute. Record it before you forget it. If you don't have your journal by your bed, then keep a piece of paper handy—with a pen.
2. It is natural for there to be some fluctuations, based upon the time you wake up, how long you have been awake, etc. But after several weeks and months, these will balance themselves out. The ideal situation would be to catch the pulse at the instant that you are awake, before the shock of an alarm clock, thoughts of work stress, etc.
3. After two weeks or so of readings, you can establish a baseline morning pulse. Take out the top two high readings and then average the readings.
4. The average is your guide. If, on a given day, the rate is 5% higher than your average, take an easy day. When the rate is 10% higher, and there is no reason for this (you woke up from an exciting dream, medication, infection, etc.), then your muscles may be tired indeed. Take a very easy day.
5. If your pulse stays high for more than a week, call your doctor to see if there is a reason for this (medication, hormones, metabolic changes, etc.).

TROUBLE-SHOOTING ACHES AND PAINS

Be sensitive to any area of the legs or feet that have been significantly sore or injured in the past. At the first sign of soreness or irritation in the following areas, read the injury chapter. It is always better to take 2-3 days off from any activity that could irritate the area, and then start back conservatively making some adaptations. With most injuries, I've found that stretching aggravates the problem. This is advice from one runner to another. For more info on injuries, treatment, etc. see the injury section of this book, *Year Round Plan* and *Galloway's Book on Running - Second Edition*.

Shins:
Soreness or pain in the front of the shin (anterior tibial area)

Note: Even after you make the corrections, shin problems often take several weeks to heal. As long as the shin problem is not a stress fracture, easy running can often allow it to heal as quickly (or more quickly) than complete layoff. In general, most runners can run when they have shin splints—they just need to stay below the threshold of further irritation.

Causes:
1. Increasing too rapidly—just walk for one week, walking with a short stride, gently.
2. Running too fast, even on one workout—when in doubt, run slower and walk slower on all runs.
3. Running or walking with a stride that is too long—shorten stride and use more of a "shuffle."

Soreness or pain at the inside of the lower leg (posterior tibial area)

Causes
1. Same three causes as in anterior tibial shin splints, above.
2. More common with runners who over-pronate. This means that they tend to roll to the inside of the foot as they push off.
3. Shoes may be too soft, allowing a floppy/pronated foot to roll inward more than usual.

Corrections:
1. Reduce stride length—shuffle more.

2. Put more walking into your run-walk ratio from the beginning.
3. If you're an over-pronator (you roll inward as you push off on the foot), get a stable, motion control shoe.
4. Ask your foot doctor if there is a foot device that can help you

Shoulder and neck muscles tired and tight
Primary Cause: leaning too far forward as you run

Other Causes:
1. Holding arms too high or too far away from the body as you run.
2. Swinging arms and shoulders too much as you run.

Corrections:
1. Use the "puppet on a string" image (detailed in the running form chapter above) about every 4-5 minutes during all runs and walks—particularly the longer ones. This is noted above in the section on posture.
2. Watch how you are holding your arms. Try to keep the arms close to the body, with shoulders relaxed.
3. Minimize the swing of your arms. Keep the hands close to the body, lightly touching your shirt or the outside of your shorts as your arms swing.

Lower back: Tight, sore, or painful after a run
Causes
1. Leaning too far forward as you run
2. Having a stride length that is too long for you

Corrections:
1. Use the "puppet on a string" image several times on all runs and walks—particularly the longer ones. This is noted above in the chapter on running form above, in the section on posture.
2. Ask a physical therapist whether some strengthening exercise can help.
3. When in doubt, shorten your stride length.
4. For more information, see *Galloway's Book on Running - Second Edition*.

Knee pain at the end of a run

Causes:
1. Not inserting enough walk breaks from the beginning of the run.
2. Stride length could be too long.
3. Doing too much exercise, too soon, particularly when beginning an exercise program.
4. When the main running muscles get tired, you will tend to wobble from side to side.

Corrections;
1. Shorten stride
2. Stay closer to the ground, using more of a shuffle
3. Monitor your mileage in a log book, and hold your increase to less than 10% a week.
4. Use more walk breaks during your run.
5. Start at a slower pace.

Behind the knee: pain, tightness, or continued soreness or weakness

Causes:
1. Stretching
2. Over striding—particularly at the end of the run

Corrections:
1. Don't stretch.
2. Keep your stride length under control.
3. Keep feet low to the ground.

Hamstrings: tightness, soreness, or pain

Causes:
1. Stretching
2. Stride length too long
3. Lifting the foot too high behind, as your leg swings back

Corrections:
1. Don't stretch.

2. Maintain a short stride, keeping the hamstring relaxed—especially at the end of the run.
3. Take more walking before starting, walk more frequently early in the run, possibly throughout the run.
4. As the leg swings behind you, let the lower leg rise no higher than a position that is parallel to horizontal before swinging forward again (don't let the leg have a big "back kick").
5. Deep tissue massage can sometimes help with this muscle group.

Quadriceps (front of the thigh): sore, tired, painful

Causes:
1. Lifting your knee too high—especially when tired
2. Using the quads to slow down going downhill—because you were running too fast

Corrections:
1. Maintain little or no knee lift—especially at the end of your run.
2. Run with a shuffle.
3. Let your stride get very short at the top of hills, and when tired—don't lengthen it.
4. If you are running too fast going down hills, keep shortening stride until you slow down, and/or take more walk breaks on the downhill.

Sore feet or lower legs

Causes:
1. Too much bounce
2. Pushing off too hard
3. Shoes don't fit correctly or are too worn out
4. Insole of shoe is worn out

Corrections:
1. Keep feet low to the ground.
2. Maintain a light touch of the feet.
3. Get a shoe check to see if your shoes are too worn.
4. You may need only a new insole.

THE CLOTHING

THERMOMETER

After years of coaching exercisers in various climates, here are my recommendations for the appropriate clothing based upon the temperature. The first layer, since it will be next to your skin, should feel comfortable, and be designed to move the moisture away from your skin. You may have to resist the temptation to buy a fashion color, but function is most important. As you try on the clothing in the store, watch for seams and extra material in areas where you will have body parts rubbing together, thousands of times during a run (armpit, between legs).

Cotton is usually not a good fabric for those who perspire a great deal. This fabric absorbs the sweat, holding it next to your skin, and increases the weight you must carry during exercise. Garments made out of fabric labeled Polypro, Coolmax, Drifit, etc., can retain enough body heat to keep you warm in winter, while releasing the extra amount. By moving moisture to the outside of the garment, these technical fabrics help you stay cooler in summer, while avoiding the winter chill.

Temperature	What to wear
14°C or 60°F and above	Tank top or singlet, and shorts
9° to 13°C or 50° to 59°F	T-shirt and shorts
5° to 8°C or 40° to 49°F	Long sleeve light weight shirt, shorts or tights (or nylon long pants) Mittens and gloves
0° to 4°C or 30° to 39°F	Long sleeve medium weight shirt, and another T shirt, tights and shorts, Socks or mittens or gloves and a hat over the ears
-4° to −1°C or 20°-29°F	Medium weight long sleeve shirt, another T shirt, tights and shorts, sox, mittens or gloves, and a hat over the ears

-8° to –3°C or 10°-19°F	Medium weight long sleeve shirt, and medium/heavy weight shirt, Tights and shorts, nylon wind suit, top and pants, socks, thick mittens And a hat over the ears
-12° to –7°C or 0°-9°F	Two medium or heavyweight long sleeve tops, thick tights, thick Thick underwear (especially for men), Medium to heavy warm up, Gloves and thick mittens, ski mask, a hat over the ears, and Vaseline covering any exposed skin.
-18° to –11°C or –15°F	Two heavyweight long sleeve tops, tights and thick tights, thick underwear (and supporter for men), thick warm up (top and pants) mittens over gloves, thick ski mask and a hat over ears, Vaseline covering any exposed skin, thicker socks on your feet and other foot protection, as needed.
Minus 20° both C & F	Add layers as needed

What not to wear

1. A heavy coat in winter. If the layer is too thick, you'll heat up, sweat excessively, and cool too much when you take it off.
2. No shirt for men in summer. Fabric that holds some of the moisture will give you more of a cooling effect as you run and walk.
3. Too much sun screen—it can interfere with sweating.
4. Socks that are too thick in summer. Your feet swell and the pressure from the socks can increase the chance of a black toenail and blisters.
5. Lime green shirt with bright pink polka dots (unless you have a lot of confidence and/or can run fast).

Special cases

Chaffing can be reduced by lycra and other fabric. Many runners have eliminated chaffing between the legs by using a lycra "bike tight" as an undergarment. These are also called "lycra shorts." There are also several skin lubricants on the market, including Glide.

Some men suffer from irritation of their nipples. Having a slick and smooth fabric across the chest will reduce this. There is now a product called Nip-Guard that has virtually eliminated this problem.

PRODUCTS

THAT ENHANCE

FITNESS

The following products will help all fitness folks. While many of these relate to running, the principles and much of the practical information apply to most activities. For more information on these, visit www.JeffGalloway.com.

Other Galloway Books: training schedules, and gifts that keep on giving—even to yourself

(Order them, autographed, from www.JeffGalloway.com)

Walking: Walkers now have a book that explains the many benefits, how to maximize them, with training programs for 5K, 10K, Half and Full Marathons. There is resource information on fat-burning, nutrition, motivation and much more.

Getting Started: This is more than a state-of-the-art book for beginners. It gently takes walkers into running, with a six month schedule that has been very successful. Also included is information on fat-burning, nutrition, motivation, and body management. This is a great gift for your friends or relatives who can be "infected" positively by running.

A Year-Round Plan: You'll find daily workouts for 52 weeks, for three levels of runners: to finish, to maximize potential, and time improvement. It has the long runs, speed sessions, drills, hill sessions, all listed, in the order needed to do a 5K, 10K, Half and Marathon during one year. Resource material is included to help with many running issues.

Galloway's Book on Running 2nd Edition: This is the best-seller among running books since 1984. Thoroughly revised and expanded in 2001, you'll find training programs for 5K, 10K, Half Marathon, with nutrition, fat-burning, walk breaks, motivation, injuries, shoes, and much more. This is a total resource book

Marathon: This has the information you need to train for the classic event. There are training programs, with details on walk breaks, long runs, marathon nutrition, mental marathon toughness and much more.

Half Marathon: This new book provides highly successful and detailed training schedules for various time goals, for this important running goal. Information is provided on nutrition, mental preparation, fluids, race day logistics and check list, and much more.

Testing Yourself: Training programs for one mile, two mile, 5K, and 1.5 mile are detailed, along with information on racing-specific information in nutrition, mental toughness, and running form. There are also some very accurate prediction tests that allow you to tell what is a realistic goal. This book has been used effectively by those who are stuck in a performance rut at 10K or longer events. By training and racing faster, you can improve running efficiency and your tolerance for waste products, like lactic acid.

The stick

This massage tool can help the muscles recover quicker. It will often speed up the recovery of muscle injuries or Iliotibial Band injuries (on the outside of the upper leg, between knee and hip). This type of device can warm up the leg muscles and reduce the aggravation of sore muscles and tendons. By promoting blood flow during and after a massage, muscle recovery time is reduced.

To use "the stick" on the calf muscle (most important in running), start each stroke at the achilles tendon and roll up the leg toward the knee. Gently roll back to the origin and continue, repeatedly. For the first five minutes, a gentle rolling motion will bring additional blood flow to the area. As you gradually increase the pressure on the calf during an "up" stroke, you'll usually find some "knots" or sore places in the muscles. Concentrate on these as you roll over them again and again, gradually breaking up the tightness. See *www.RunInjuryFree.com* for more info on this.

Foam roller—self massage for I-T Band, Hip, etc.

This cylinder of dense foam is about six inches in diameter and about one foot long. I've not seen any mode of treatment for Iliotibial band injury that has been more effective. For best effect, put the roller on the floor, and lie on your side so that the irritated I-T band area is on top of the roller. As your body weight presses down on the roller, roll up and down on the area of the leg you want to treat. Roll gently for 2-3 minutes and then apply more pressure as desired. This is actually a deep tissue massage that you can perform on yourself. For I-T band, I recommend rolling it before and after running. See www.RunInjuryFree.com for more info on this product.

Cryo-Cup—best tool for ice massage

Rubbing with a chunk of ice on a sore area (when near the skin) is very powerful therapy. I know of hundreds of cases of Achilles tendon problems that have been healed by this method. The Cryo-Cup is a very convenient device for ice massage. The plastic cup has a plastic ring that sits on top of it. Fill it up with water, and then freeze. When you have an ache or pain that is close to the skin, take the product out of the freezer, pour warm water over the outside of the cup to release it, and hold onto the plastic handle like an ice "popcicle." Rub constantly up and down the affected area for about 15 minutes, until the tendon (etc) is numb. When finished, fill the cup and place in the freezer. In my experience, rubbing with a plastic bag of ice—or a frozen gel product—does no good at all in most cases.

YOU CAN DO IT—motivational audio CD

Put this in your car player as you drive to your run. You'll be motivated by the stories as you learn the strategies and methods that have allowed runners to deal with the negative messages of the left side of the brain—and push to their potential.

Endurox Excel

Many runners over 50 years old have told me that they have noticed a significantly faster muscle rebound when using this product. An hour before a long or hard workout, I take two of these Excel pills. Among the anti-oxidants is the active ingredient from gensing: ciwega. Research has shown that recovery time is reduced when this product is taken. I also use it when my legs have been more tired than usual for 2-3 days in a row.

Accelerade

This sports drink has a patented formula shown to improve recovery. Drinking it before and after prolonged, dehydrating workouts also helps to improve hydration. I recommend having a half gallon container of Accelerade in the refrigerator. Drink 4-8 oz every 1-2 hours, throughout the day. Best time to "top off" your fluid levels is within 24 hours before a long run. Prime time for replacing fluids is during the 24 hour period after a long run. Many runners have 32 oz or so in a thermos, for sipping during walk breaks in a prolonged speed training session. I suggest adding about 25% more water than recommended.

Research has also shown that drinking Accelerade about 30 min before running can get the body's startup fuel (glycogen) activated more effectively, and may conserve the limited supply of this crucial fuel.

Endurox R4

This product has almost "cult following" status among runners. In fact, the research shows that the 4-1 ratio of carbohydrate to protein helps to reload the muscle glycogen more quickly (when consumed within 30 min of the finish of a hard or long workout). This means that the muscles feel bouncy and ready to do what you can do, sooner. There are other anti-oxidants in R4 that speed recovery.

Jeff Galloway's Training Journal

Some type of journal is recommended to organize, and track, your training plan. *Jeff Galloway's Training Journal* can be ordered from www.JeffGalloway.com, autographed. It simplifies the process, with places to fill in information for each day. There is also space for recording the unexpected thoughts and experiences that make so many runs come alive again as we read them.

Your journal allows you to take control over the organization of your training components. As you plan ahead and then compare notes afterward, you are empowered to learn from your experience, and make positive changes.

Galloway PC Coach—interactive software: This software will not only set up a marathon training program, it will help you to stay on track. As you log in, you're told if your training is not what it should be for that day. Sort through various training components quickly, and often find reasons why you are tired or have more aches and pains, etc.

Vitamins

I now believe that most runners need a good vitamin to boost the immune system and resist infection. There is some evidence that getting the proper vitamin mix can also speed recovery. The vitamin line I use is called Cooper Complete. Dr. Kenneth Cooper (founder of the Cooper Clinic and the Aerobics Institute), is behind this product. In the process of compiling the most formidable body of research on exercise and long-term health I've seen anywhere, he found that certain vitamins play important roles.
www.coopercomplete.com

Buffered salt tablets—to reduce cramping

If your muscles cramp on long or hard runs, due to salt depletion, this type of product may help greatly. The buffered sodium and potassium tablets get into the system more quickly. Be sure to ask your doctor if this product is OK for you (those with high blood pressure, especially). If you are taking a statin drug for cholesterol, and are cramping, it is doubtful that this will help. Ask your doctor about adjusting the medication before long runs.

Advisors:
John Cantwell, M.D.
Diana Twiggs, M.D.
Jeffrey Kopland, MD, MPH
Ruth Parker, M.D.
Julie Gazmararian, MPH, PhD
Nancy Clark, MS, RD
Mike Pratt, MD
Russell Pate, PhD

Photo & Illustration Credits

Cover Photos:	getty images/Digital Vision
Cover Design:	Jens Vogelsang
Inside Photos:	p. 211 Bakke-Svensson/WTC
	getty images/Digital Vision